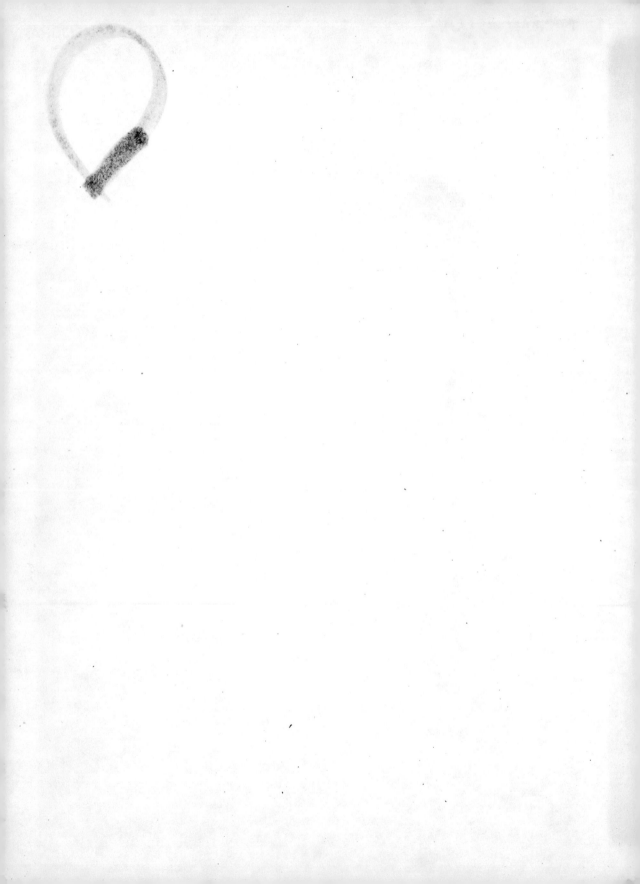

EDDIE
MURPHY

EDDIE MURPHY

Deborah A. Wilburn

CHELSEA HOUSE PUBLISHERS
New York   Philadelphia

Chelsea House Publishers
Editorial Director   Richard Rennert
Executive Managing Editor   Karyn Gullen Browne
Executive Editor   Sean Dolan
Copy Chief   Philip Koslow
Picture Editor   Adrian G. Allen
Art Director   Nora Wertz
Manufacturing Director   Gerald Levine
Systems Manager   Lindsey Ottman
Production Coordinator   Marie Claire Cebrián-Ume

Black Americans of Achievement
Senior Editor   Richard Rennert

Staff for EDDIE MURPHY
Copy Editor   Danielle Janusz
Editorial Assistants   Nicole Greenblatt, Joy Sanchez
Designer   Ghila Krajzman
Picture Researcher   Wendy P. Wills
Cover Illustrator   Janet Hamlin

First Printing

1 3 5 7 9 8 6 4 2

Library of Congress Cataloging-in-Publication Data
Wilburn, Deborah A.
    Eddie Murphy/Deborah A. Wilburn
        p. cm.—(Black Americans of achievement)
    Includes bibliographical references and index.
  Summary: Discusses the professional and personal life of the
well-known comedian.
   ISBN   0-7910-1879-2
           0-7910-1908-X (pbk.)
   1. Murphy, Eddie—Juvenile literature. 2. Comedians—United
States—Biography—Juvenile literature. 3. Entertainers—United
States—Biography—Juvenile literature.
[1. Murphy, Eddie. 2. Comedians. 3. Entertainers.
4. Afro-Americans—Biography.] I. Title. II. Series.
PN2287.M815W55 1993   92-31310
792.7'028'092—dc20   CIP
[B]

CONTENTS

—◀◖◗▶—

BLACK AMERICANS OF ACHIEVEMENT

HENRY AARON
baseball great

KAREEM ABDUL-JABBAR
basketball great

RALPH ABERNATHY
civil rights leader

ALVIN AILEY
choreographer

MUHAMMAD ALI
heavyweight champion

RICHARD ALLEN
religious leader and social activist

MAYA ANGELOU
author

LOUIS ARMSTRONG
musician

ARTHUR ASHE
tennis great

JOSEPHINE BAKER
entertainer

JAMES BALDWIN
author

BENJAMIN BANNEKER
scientist and mathematician

AMIRI BARAKA
poet and playwright

COUNT BASIE
bandleader and composer

ROMARE BEARDEN
artist

JAMES BECKWOURTH
frontiersman

MARY MCLEOD BETHUNE
educator

JULIAN BOND
civil rights leader and politician

GWENDOLYN BROOKS
poet

JIM BROWN
football great

RALPH BUNCHE
diplomat

STOKELY CARMICHAEL
civil rights leader

GEORGE WASHINGTON CARVER
botanist

RAY CHARLES
musician

CHARLES CHESNUTT
author

JOHN COLTRANE
musician

BILL COSBY
entertainer

PAUL CUFFE
merchant and abolitionist

COUNTEE CULLEN
poet

BENJAMIN DAVIS, SR., AND BENJAMIN DAVIS, JR.
military leaders

SAMMY DAVIS, JR.
entertainer

FATHER DIVINE
religious leader

FREDERICK DOUGLASS
abolitionist editor

CHARLES DREW
physician

W. E. B. DU BOIS
scholar and activist

PAUL LAURENCE DUNBAR
poet

KATHERINE DUNHAM
dancer and choreographer

DUKE ELLINGTON
bandleader and composer

RALPH ELLISON
author

JULIUS ERVING
basketball great

JAMES FARMER
civil rights leader

ELLA FITZGERALD
singer

MARCUS GARVEY
black nationalist leader

JOSH GIBSON
baseball great

DIZZY GILLESPIE
musician

WHOOPI GOLDBERG
entertainer

ALEX HALEY
author

PRINCE HALL
social reformer

MATTHEW HENSON
explorer

CHESTER HIMES
author

BILLIE HOLIDAY
singer

LENA HORNE
entertainer

LANGSTON HUGHES
poet

ZORA NEALE HURSTON
author

JESSE JACKSON
civil rights leader and politicia

MICHAEL JACKSON
entertainer

JACK JOHNSON
heavyweight champion

JAMES WELDON JOHNSON
author

MAGIC JOHNSON
basketball great

SCOTT JOPLIN
composer

BARBARA JORDAN
politician

MICHAEL JORDAN
basketball great

CORETTA SCOTT KING
civil rights leader

MARTIN LUTHER KING, JR.
civil rights leader

LEWIS LATIMER
scientist

SPIKE LEE
filmmaker

CARL LEWIS
champion athlete

JOE LOUIS
heavyweight champion

RONALD McNAIR
astronaut

MALCOLM X
militant black leader

THURGOOD MARSHAL
Supreme Court justice

TONI MORRISON
author

ELIJAH MUHAMMAD
religious leader

EDDIE MURPHY
entertainer

JESSE OWENS
champion athlete

SATCHEL PAIGE
baseball great

CHARLIE PARKER
musician

GORDON PARKS
photographer

ROSA PARKS
civil rights leader

SIDNEY POITIER
actor

ADAM CLAYTON
POWELL, JR.
political leader

COLIN POWELL
military leader

LEONTYNE PRICE
opera singer

A. PHILIP RANDOLPH
labor leader

PAUL ROBESON
singer and actor

JACKIE ROBINSON
baseball great

DIANA ROSS
entertainer

BILL RUSSELL
basketball great

JOHN RUSSWURM
publisher

SOJOURNER TRUTH
antislavery activist

HARRIET TUBMAN
antislavery activist

NAT TURNER
slave revolt leader

DENMARK VESEY
slave revolt leader

ALICE WALKER
author

MADAM C. J. WALKER
entrepreneur

BOOKER T. WASHINGTON
educator and racial spokesman

IDA WELLS-BARNETT
civil rights leader

WALTER WHITE
civil rights leader

OPRAH WINFREY
entertainer

STEVIE WONDER
musician

RICHARD WRIGHT
author

ON ACHIEVEMENT

Coretta Scott King

BEFORE YOU BEGIN this book, I hope you will ask yourself what the word *excellence* means to you. I think that it's a question we should all ask, and keep asking as we grow older and change. Because the truest answer to it should never change. When you think of excellence, perhaps you think of success at work; or of becoming wealthy; or meeting the right person, getting married, and having a good family life.

Those important goals are worth striving for, but there is a better way to look at excellence. As Martin Luther King, Jr., said in one of his last sermons, "I want you to be first in love. I want you to be first in moral excellence. I want you to be first in generosity. If you want to be important, wonderful. If you want to be great, wonderful. But recognize that he who is greatest among you shall be your servant."

My husband, Martin Luther King, Jr., knew that the true meaning of achievement is service. When I met him, in 1952, he was already ordained as a Baptist preacher and was working toward a doctoral degree at Boston University. I was studying at the New England Conservatory and dreamed of accomplishments in music. We married a year later, and after I graduated the following year we moved to Montgomery, Alabama. We didn't know it then, but our notions of achievement were about to undergo a dramatic change.

You may have read or heard about what happened next. What began with the boycott of a local bus line grew into a national movement, and by the time he was assassinated in 1968 my husband had fashioned a black movement powerful enough to shatter forever the practice of racial segregation. What you may not have read about is where he got his method for resisting injustice without compromising his religious beliefs.

He adopted the strategy of nonviolence from a man of a different race, who lived in a different country, and even practiced a different religion. The man was Mahatma Gandhi, the great leader of India, who devoted his life to serving humanity in the spirit of love and nonviolence. It was in these principles that Martin discovered his method for social reform. More than anything else, those two principles were the key to his achievements.

This book is about black Americans who served society through the excellence of their achievements. It forms a part of the rich history of black men and women in America—a history of stunning accomplishments in every field of human endeavor, from literature and art to science, industry, education, diplomacy, athletics, jurisprudence, even polar exploration.

Not all of the people in this history had the same ideals, but I think you will find something that all of them had in common. Like Martin Luther King, Jr., they all decided to become "drum majors" and serve humanity. In that principle—whether it was expressed in books, inventions, or song—they found something outside themselves to use as a goal and a guide. Something that showed them a way to serve others, instead of only living for themselves.

Reading the stories of these courageous men and women not only helps us discover the principles that we will use to guide our own lives but also teaches us about our black heritage and about America itself. It is crucial for us to know the heroes and heroines of our history and to realize that the price we paid in our struggle for equality in America was dear. But we must also understand that we have gotten as far as we have partly because America's democratic system and ideals made it possible.

We are still struggling with racism and prejudice. But the great men and women in this series are a tribute to the spirit of our democratic ideals and the system in which they have flourished. And that makes their stories special and worth knowing. ◆◊◆

1

"JUST GIVE ME A CHANCE"

"**H**EH. HEH. HEH."

It was his laugh that always cracked up audiences the most. No matter how incisive the put-down, no matter how sharp the stereotype Eddie Murphy was blasting out of the water, his hyenalike laugh and the gleam in his eyes were enough to erase any misunderstanding that he was being malicious or mean. Far from it. Murphy's trademark laugh was his way of reminding audiences that he was going for *their* laugh.

And he got it. Beginning in 1981, when he started his second season on the nation's top-rated, late-night comedy program, the New York City–based "Saturday Night Live," Murphy not only got the laughs; he practically owned the show. With his searing impersonations of such celebrities as comedian Bill Cosby, civil rights leader Jesse Jackson, and music stars James Brown and Stevie Wonder, Murphy made an indelible mark on late-night television.

The hilarious characters he developed on the program, from a grumpy Gumby to the soft-voiced Mr. Robinson, host of a ghetto version of the popular children's show "Mr. Rogers' Neighborhood," kept audiences howling and begging for more. In fact, at the tender age of 20, Murphy was not only America's

"Success is pure faith in yourself and God," according to Eddie Murphy, one of the entertainment industry's superstars. "You've got one life. I say, you go for what you want."

crown prince of comedy, he was on his way to international superstardom.

But the road was not easy. It took guts and perseverance for Murphy to even get a shot at auditioning for the Not Ready for Prime Time Players, as members of the "Saturday Night Live" cast were called. But once he got the chance, he seized the moment for all it was worth. And why not? It was an opportunity Murphy had been rehearsing for his entire life.

In 1980, when Murphy first auditioned for "Saturday Night Live," the show was entering its sixth season on NBC. Featuring irreverent, off-the-wall skits and commentaries that changed the face of American comedy, the program had served as a springboard for a handful of comedians who became overnight sensations. By 1980, however, the original producer, Lorne Michaels, and cast members had decided to call it quits despite the show's immense popularity. Many of them were moving on to Hollywood, where they would achieve enormous success in the film industry, most notably the Not Ready for Prime Time Players Dan Aykroyd, John Belushi, Chevy Chase, and Bill Murray.

After these "Saturday Night Live" veterans relinquished their spots in the cast, scores of comedians, including Murphy, vied for a chance to ascend to the NBC studio on the 17th floor of 30 Rockefeller Plaza to audition for the show. When Murphy received word that Jean Doumanian, the new producer, was looking for a male performer and that she "wouldn't object at all if that person happened to be black," he became especially determined. At the time, the 19-year-old comic was working stand-up in small nightclubs on Long Island, where he had been raised.

Murphy had been honing his stand-up skills in front of live audiences since he was 15. He mainly performed solo, although for a while he had teamed

A man of many talents, Murphy is first and foremost a stand-up comic. He launched his show business career in the mid-1970s, when he performed stand-up comedy routines in small suburban nightclubs.

The teenage Murphy at the start of a brilliant career, when he was on his way to becoming a featured player on the highly popular "Saturday Night Live" television show.

up with a couple of white comedians in a novelty group called the Identical Triplets. It was one of the Triplets, Bob Nelson, who helped Murphy make the quantum leap from performing in the sleepy Long Island suburbs to appearing at the Comic Strip, a Manhattan club where many comedy stars were born.

At the Comic Strip, untested talents could get onstage and try out their material on amateur night, which was held once a week. With any luck, these fledgling comedians would catch the attention of the club owners, Richard Tienken and Robert Wachs, and be invited to perform on the weekend. And with a bit more luck and talent, the comics would get a chance to perform regularly. Nelson, whose appearances at the Comic Strip had been well received, put in a good word for Murphy, and Eddie was given a shot at performing one amateur night.

Murphy mainly did impressions during his first Comic Strip appearance. And even though comedians doing impressions were a dime a dozen, Tienken and Wachs noticed that the teenager's act appealed to the audience. "From his earliest appearances," Wachs remembered, "Eddie had an amazing confidence on stage, a tremendous smile, an infectious laugh, a vulnerability, a likeability."

The two club owners were sufficiently interested in Murphy to work with him on improving his timing, delivery, and material. Although they did not manage any of the other talented performers who crossed the club's threshold, they agreed to represent Murphy when he asked them.

Murphy was performing at another of Tienken and Wachs's comedy clubs, the Comic Strip in Fort Lauderdale, Florida, when he received word that "Saturday Night Live" was looking for an "ethnic" comedian. He immediately returned to New York, only to learn that the auditions for a black performer had already been held and that the producer was leaning toward hiring a comic she had already seen.

The news did not stop Eddie. He immediately besieged Neil Levy, the show's talent coordinator, with phone calls, begging him for an audition. Murphy sometimes called him three times a day to say what a great comedian he was and how badly he needed the job. All he wanted, Murphy said, was a chance. Finally, Levy relented.

When Murphy went to the 17th-floor studio to audition for Levy, he did a routine about three guys hanging out on a Harlem street corner: the short guy

For most of his first season on "Saturday Night Live," Murphy was just another face in the crowd. But he eventually distinguished himself from the rest of the show's cast, which included (from left to right) Tony Rosato, Tim Kazurinsky, Christine Ebersole, Robin Duke, Mary Gross, and Joe Piscopo.

mouths off, provoking the other two into fighting each other. Levy was so impressed that *he* began pestering the show's producer to see Murphy perform. Doumanian told Levy to have the young comic audition for her associate.

When Murphy returned to the 17th floor, he performed not only for the producer's associate; in the hope of garnering more staff support, he did his act for anyone he and Levy could get to listen. At one point, a script was pulled from the show's files—a job interview sketch that had been written for Chevy Chase to perform with Murphy's idol, Richard Pryor, when Pryor was guest host of "Saturday Night Live." Joe Piscopo, who had already been hired as a Not Ready for Prime Time Player, volunteered to read the script with Murphy.

The two comedians ran through the sketch, and Piscopo instantly became a Murphy fan. "Eddie took charge [of the piece]," Piscopo recalled. "I said, 'This guy is *great*.'"

Murphy's never-say-die attitude was beginning to pay off, for Doumanian agreed to see him. Although she was impressed by his subsequent performance, the producer said she was concerned about his youth and inexperience. Levy and other staff members argued that the 19-year-old's raw talent would make up for any lack of experience.

After six auditions, Murphy was finally hired, but not as a regular cast member. Instead, he was made a featured player, earning $750 per show—about 15 percent of the amount that the other cast members received. In effect, he was a glorified extra.

Murphy refused to believe the producer's claim that he was too inexperienced to be granted a regular spot on the show. "I figured they hired me," he said later, "so that if someone wrote a letter asking, 'How come you got no brothers on the show?' they could point to me." Garrett Morris, the original black cast member who had left "Saturday Night Live" at the end of the previous season, had been the show's lone black performer. And now that Morris was gone, Murphy was the token black. He maintained, "They just threw me in there to be the black guy on the show."

There the similarities between the two comics ended, for Murphy was determined not to follow in Morris's footsteps. Morris had never received much recognition on the show and was often cast in embarrassing stereotypical roles. He also appeared on the program dressed in drag, impersonating black female entertainers. Murphy's intent was to avoid Morris's fate.

Murphy faced an uphill battle in making his mark on "Saturday Night Live." He got very little air time during his first season on the show. Doumanian had instructed the program's writers to churn out material for the regular cast members because "they should be established first." Her instructions meant that no material was written for Murphy.

Doumanian's approach turned out to be a blessing in disguise for Murphy. The first shows of the season under the new producer bombed. The material was not funny, nor were the majority of the actors. Critics panned the show, and the ratings declined steadily.

Comedian Steve Martin (left) and the "Saturday Night Live" cast congratulate Murphy in 1982 following the announcement that he had become a full-fledged member of the show.

As the season wore on, Piscopo, with whom Murphy had become fast friends, was given air time to develop some of his characters to try to salvage the show. Meanwhile, Murphy was stuck biding his time on the 17th floor, calmly eating cheeseburgers and observing everyone around him. Sometimes—to the chagrin of his fellow cast members—he would let loose with a dead-on-the-money impersonation of one of them. Ever confident, he started autographing the walls with the words *Eddie Murphy #1*. These actions did little to endear him to his fellow performers, but Murphy did not care. He was becoming increasingly impatient for a chance to perform.

Murphy appeared on the program for the first time as an extra. His brief role called for him to sit on a couch during a cocktail party routine, without speaking any lines. "If only they'd give me a chance," he lamented to a friend. "I'd make it *so* funny."

Whenever Murphy asked Doumanian when he would be allowed to make a contribution, she would tell him he was still learning and would have to wait a while. Murphy continued to badger her, until the producer told him to think of a bit to do on Weekend Update, the show's weekly spoof of the news.

Murphy grabbed his chance. By this time, he had become friendly with two of the show's writers, Barry Blaustein and David Sheffield, and he approached them about developing a routine to perform on Weekend Update. Blaustein mentioned a recent news item in which a Cleveland judge had ruled that high school basketball teams had to have at least two white players on their roster to ensure racial balance. Murphy thought the item over and came back the next day with the character of Raheem Abdul Muhammed, a militant black who expresses outrage at the ruling. The writers agreed that Murphy's bit was terrific, and he was penciled into the Weekend Update segment.

On the night of the show, the teenager was nervous but excited as he stood in the wings and waited to go on. "The kids at Roosevelt High aren't going to believe this," he whispered to Piscopo, who was standing next to him. Moments later, Piscopo, playing the part of Weekend Update's sports announcer, mentioned the Cleveland judge's ruling and then introduced his guest commentator, Raheem Abdul Muhammed, who immediately began to rant about the judge moving in on "blacks' territory."

"Yo, baby," Murphy's Raheem character said. "Look, I bin a junior at Cleveland High for seven years now, and let me tell you that this is the most disgusting thing y'all have pulled up to date. I mean, we ain't got much, at least let us have basketball. Is nothing sacred? Any time we get something good going, y'all move in on it. . . . I don't see no judge saying that every two bathroom attendants have to be white! All I'm saying is y'all stick to playing hockey and polo and we'll stay in the courts."

Murphy concluded his bit by saying, "I mean, if God wanted whites to be equal with blacks, everyone would have one of these!" With that, he reached under the Weekend Update desk, pulled out a monstrous radio, and, with the boom box playing, stared defiantly into the camera.

No other routine that season had gotten bigger laughs. It became immediately clear to just about everyone connected with "Saturday Night Live" that Murphy should appear regularly on the program. And with him contributing more ideas to the show as the weeks went by, the writers responded by including him in more of their sketches. After all, he and Piscopo were the only ones who were getting any consistent laughs.

Then two things happened to signal that Murphy had truly arrived. One night, with the show running five minutes short—there was not enough material to fill the allotted air time—Levy convinced Doumanian to let the young comic fill the time by doing a bit from his stand-up act. Pushed into the spotlight on short notice, Murphy did his three-guys-on-a-Harlem-street-corner routine. It won the audience over, just as it had won the producers over during his audition.

The second major development came two weeks later, when Doumanian again sent Murphy onstage by himself. This time, however, it was to announce that he had been promoted: he was now a full-fledged regular cast member. The audience in the NBC studio roared its approval. In the space of just a few months, he had made the tremendous leap from Long Island's nightclub circuit to a prime spot on television's most popular and enduring comedy show.

And that was just the beginning of Eddie Murphy's remarkable career as an entertainer, one that would constantly leave his fans clamoring for more of his comic genius. •◖•

2

"YOU HAD TO BE QUICK"

EDWARD REGAN MURPHY was born on April 3, 1961, in Brooklyn, New York. The second of Lillian and Charles Murphy's two children—he was a year younger than his brother, Charlie—Eddie spent his early childhood in a predominantly black, lower-middle-class neighborhood in the Bushwick section of Brooklyn. Throughout most of that period, his home was a cramped apartment.

Both of Eddie's parents held jobs. Lillian Murphy was employed as a telephone operator, and her husband was a New York City transit police officer who worked on weekends at local night spots as an amateur comedian and emcee. Like his youngest son, Charles, Sr., possessed a great sense of humor. But Eddie barely got to know the man whose keen wit he apparently inherited. When Eddie was three years old, his parents separated, and his father moved out of the apartment.

The breakup of his parents' marriage marked the beginning of an extremely difficult period in Eddie's life. Without his father around, money became tighter than ever. To make matters worse, his mother fell gravely ill and had to be hospitalized. When that

The budding young comic as a high school student, about the time that he told one of his teachers, "I'm going to be bigger than Bob Hope."

23

happened, Eddie and Charlie were sent to live in a foster home for a while.

"Those were baaaad days," Eddie Murphy recalled. He and his brother were taken care of by a woman who was "a kind of black Nazi," Eddie said. "Staying with her was probably the reason I became a comedian."

But that was not the only reason. Eddie, in fact, was born with a gift for comedy. According to his mother, he never had to be encouraged to be funny. He always possessed a highly charged sense of humor.

Eddie refined his comic gifts by watching cartoons for hours and absorbing the mannerisms of such animated characters as Bugs Bunny and Tom and Jerry. Later, he would do perfect imitations of their voices. "My mother says I never talked in my own voice—always cartoon characters. Dudley Do-Right, Bullwinkle," the comedian said years later. "I used to do Sylvester the Cat (thufferin' thuccotash) all the time. I could get my brother Charlie mad by doing Bela Lugosi [an actor noted for his portrayal of Dracula]. Get him in trouble. I was that kind of kid."

But Eddie never got his brother—or himself—into serious trouble. His pranks, such as impersonating the school principal, were mainly extensions of his irrepressible sense of humor. By his mother's account, Eddie was a well-behaved, sensitive child. "I'll never forget when he was six or seven and I would spank him," she said. "He would say, 'I know why you spanked me, Mommy. You spanked me because you love me.' "

After Charles, Sr., moved out of the apartment, Eddie never had regular contact with his father, although the youngster sometimes saw him on weekends, when the elder Murphy would take him to the movies. Because these visits occurred infrequently, Eddie never got much of an opportunity to get to know his father. "People tell me I walk like my father, hold my head like my father," he said. "But I don't have a 'Once my father did this' story."

Any chance to get to know his father better was wiped away on Labor Day weekend, 1969, when Charles Murphy was stabbed to death by his girlfriend. "I never got all the logistics," Eddie said. "It was supposed to be one of those crimes of passion: an 'If I can't have you, then no one else will' kind of deal." Eddie Murphy has since referred to his father's death as the greatest tragedy in his own life.

Eddie, however, did not grow up lacking a strong father figure. Eddie's mother befriended Vernon Lynch, who worked as a foreman at a Breyer's ice-cream factory on Long Island. Lynch, who was also an amateur boxer and part-time boxing instructor, eventually became Eddie and Charlie's stepfather and raised them as his own sons. Vernon, Sr., and Lillian also gave the two boys a half brother, Vernon, Jr.

In 1970, Eddie's family moved out of Brooklyn and settled in a two-story, three-bedroom shingled

Voted one of the most popular students at Roosevelt High School, Murphy (right) was also one of the funniest. By his senior year, he was entertaining his classmates in packed assemblies.

ranch house. It was located in the largely black middle-class suburb of Roosevelt, a town in the middle of Long Island. The move out of the inner city was a positive one for the family, for it meant living in a nice, roomy house instead of a cramped apartment. But the move was hard on nine-year-old Eddie. He had to leave behind his old friends and his old neighborhood, and the kids in Roosevelt did not accept him right away. He was forced to put up with teasing and "ranking"—a witty form of insult—from the other children, who were at first wary of the newcomer.

"I'd spent nine years making myself into Mr. Cool," Eddie Murphy later said of his early days in Brooklyn. But when he moved to the suburbs, "right away I became Mr. Jerk. The kids ranked on me, and I had to rank back. They called me 'Peas' because for a whole year I wouldn't comb my hair. It rolled up in these little balls—you know, the Sidney Poitier look. They'd tease girls about me, too: 'Peas is your boyfriend, Peas is your boyfriend.' When they'd start on me with 'Peas, why is your hair . . . ,' I'd go 'Why is your mother's hair . . .' Like that. You had to be quick."

And Eddie was quick, as the kids in the new neighborhood found out. He was as good, if not better, at ranking than they were. Although Eddie was never one to hang out on the streets or join a gang, he soon became popular in his new school and formed firm friendships, some of which have lasted to this day. His sharp sense of humor and ability to think on his feet helped him win the respect—and later, the admiration—of his classmates.

While Eddie continued to mimic cartoon charac-ters, he added impersonations of comedians such as Laurel and Hardy and Jerry Lewis to his repertoire. In fact, a large part of Eddie Murphy's talent for imitation can be attributed to his powers of perception. Even in grade school, he had the uncanny ability to observe people and television characters and then reproduce their manner of speech and behavior perfectly.

Comedy was not Eddie's only talent. He was also gifted musically, although he stopped taking guitar lessons as a child because he said that playing the instrument hurt his fingers. He enjoyed drawing—scraps of paper covered with his artwork littered the house—and puppets were his passion. When he was 11 years old, he begged for a ventriloquist's dummy for Christmas and got his wish.

In junior high school, Eddie's interests were varied, ranging from sports to those activities that later formed the bedrock of his life as a performer. He once signed a school book report "Eddie Murphy, singer, writer, actor, comedian, impersonist, boxer, basketball player, football player, genius and a gift from God to all womenkind. P.S. I'm not conceided, I'm just not a lier." One word most notably missing from his list was "scholar." Eddie did not like to study and spent as little time as possible doing his schoolwork.

Whenever Eddie was not watching television, working on his impersonations, or ranking with his friends, he enjoyed playing sports. "Eddie didn't like contact sports," his mother recalled. "He played baseball, but basically he didn't want to get hurt." His family joked that Eddie was a borderline hypochondriac because he made such a fuss over the smallest knicks and cuts. Vernon, Jr., for one, would laugh as his older brother attended to his scrapes. "He would wash it thoroughly, put Mercurochrome on it," Vernon, Jr., said, "and add Band-Aid after Band-Aid."

Even though Eddie avoided contact sports as much as possible, there was one activity he could not escape: boxing. His stepfather insisted on giving lessons to all the boys in the family basement, where there were always at least two sets of boxing gloves ready to be used in an impromptu sparring session. Vernon Lynch believed Eddie had promise as a fighter, but the youngster simply did not like the sport. "I'm just not a fighter, Pop," Eddie would protest. Still, he could not win a total reprieve. Whenever Eddie or one of his brothers got out of line, Vernon would order the errant child into the basement to spar a few rounds.

Eddie's love affair with television continued throughout junior high school. "I Love Lucy," "The Honeymooners," and "Batman" were added to his daily diet of television viewing. John Landis, who later directed Eddie Murphy in *Trading Places* and *Coming to America*, once told *Time* magazine that he believed Eddie's unique point of view was rooted in his habit of watching television. "I grew up hooked on TV," said Landis, "but Eddie *is* TV. His world experience comes from the tube."

Comedienne Lucille Ball stands alongside costar Desi Arnaz on the set of "I Love Lucy," one of the many television shows that Murphy watched religiously while he was growing up. Television viewing, in fact, influenced many of his ideas about comedy.

Eddie never mustered a similar enthusiasm for his schoolwork. He attended summer school after the eighth grade to keep up with his classmates—and did so every year until he graduated from high school. His poor grades had become a constant source of concern to his mother. She knew Eddie was bright, and she could not understand why he would not apply himself and earn higher marks. Lillian Murphy wanted her son to have a solid education so he could go to college and get a good job. But he had other goals and dreams in mind.

Eddie's interest in becoming a comedian grew while he was a student at Roosevelt High School. Whereas most of his peers would spend their free time after school shooting hoops and trying to emulate Roosevelt High's most celebrated graduate, basketball star Julius ("Dr. J") Erving, Eddie would return home and head for the family room in the basement. There he worked on his impersonations of his two idols, singer Elvis Presley and comedian Richard Pryor, as well as Bill Cosby, Stevie Wonder, and vocalist Al Green. Down in the paneled basement that had been finished by his stepfather, Eddie entered a world of his own, a world where he was a stand-up comic, a star, entertaining his fans with jokes and impersonations.

Sometimes Eddie practiced his imitations in front of a mirror. On other occasions, he would don a gold lamé coat given to him by an uncle, put Elvis Presley's *Live from Madison Square Garden* album on the stereo, and lip-synch each song while copying Presley's gyrating movements. According to Eddie, Elvis was the greatest entertainer who had ever lived. "I thought he had more presence and charisma than anybody who ever existed."

One of the most embarrassing moments in Eddie's life came while he was working on his Elvis routine. One day, thinking he was alone in the basement, he launched into his act. Ten minutes later, Charlie emerged from a hiding place. "'You're crazy, man. Really crazy,'" Eddie recalled his brother saying. "He wanted to know what I was rehearsing for. I had no answer."

The answer to Charlie's question began to reveal itself on July 9, 1976. That was the date of Eddie Murphy's first gig. He and a friend (who was also well known for his skill at ranking) were asked to host a talent show at the Roosevelt Youth Center, where they often gathered with other neighborhood kids.

Eddie, who was then in the 10th grade, was excited about hosting the show. Not only did he crack jokes between acts, he performed his own routine. He put on an Al Green record and lip-synched the words, imitating Green's style and throwing in some of the pelvic moves he had rehearsed in his family's basement. The girls in the audience went crazy, and as far as Eddie was concerned, his future was set. "The truth is," he said later, "I knew what I was put here to do. . . . I wanted to be in show biz."

After the talent show, Eddie and his buddy decided to form their own band. But their repertoire was limited, so Eddie began to do comic bits between songs to fill out the act. The audience loved everything he did, and suddenly he was known as a singer, top ranker, and the funniest kid in school. "In high school, I used to give assemblies," he recalled. "One time I did a show for the six grades over three days. My band played, and afterward, I did an hour of material about the school. Impressions of teachers, students, hall monitors. There were routines about smoking marijuana behind the school, getting caught by the truant officer, cutting class, getting detention and gym class. By the third day, people were sitting in the aisles."

A short time later, an appearance on a local cable television show helped the teenager become a neighborhood celebrity. After that, he decided to drop music and focus solely on his first love, comedy. He performed stand-up whenever and wherever he could, including gong shows (talent shows where anyone could get onstage and perform) at the local nightclubs.

Fifteen-year-old Eddie Murphy proved popular with the audiences. And even though he made only $25 to $50 a week, he received something far more valuable than money. Performing onstage in front of a live audience enabled him to work on his timing and polish his routines.

Rock-and-roll singer Elvis Presley was among the entertainers whom Murphy enjoyed imitating in the privacy of the family basement. These rehearsal sessions eventually helped the teenage comic develop into a master impersonator.

The wildly inventive Richard Pryor was the comedian who probably influenced Murphy's humor the most. Accordingly, Murphy received a great thrill when he later got the chance to costar with his idol in the movie Harlem Nights.

Lillian Lynch drove her son from show to show and was proud of his success. But what she did not realize was that after these performances he snuck off to after-hours joints, "getting paid," she learned later, "for telling jokes with four-letter words." She became aware of what Eddie was doing only after one of her husband's co-workers stopped in at one of the night spots, caught the act, and told Vernon about it.

Eddie never used off-color language around the house, and his mother and stepfather did not approve of him using it in nightclubs. Still, the four-letter words became an integral part of his act. Like Richard Pryor, whose comedy albums were peppered with obscenities, the budding comic felt that foul-mouthed humor was what people wanted to hear. He pointed out, "You'll never hear anyone between eleven and twenty-eight going, 'That Eddie Murphy uses too much profanity.'"

By the time Eddie was 17, his income had increased to an average of $300 a week—a large amount of money for a teenager who was still in high school. The better he got at stand-up comedy, however, the worse his grades became. "I used to come home with report cards . . . with zeroes on them and 50s and 60s," he remembered. "My mother would say, 'What's wrong with you?' I'd say, 'I'm going to be famous, Ma.'"

Staying up late every night to perform left Eddie with little time and energy to do his schoolwork, and he found any excuse to cut his classes. "You could usually find me in the lunchroom," he said, "trying out my routines on the kids to perform them in clubs later that night." Although his audience of peers appreciated his act, his teachers did not—and they let him know it. Eddie refused to be cowed. One time, he answered back to a disapproving social studies teacher, "I'm going to be bigger than Bob Hope."

This prophecy indeed came true only a few years later; yet Eddie's future certainly looked bleak during his sophomore year in high school, when his grades fell so low that he was told he would have to repeat the 10th grade. Being left back dealt an enormous blow to his ego. "As vain as I was, I can't tell you what that did to me," Eddie said. "I went to summer school, to night school and I doubled up on classes." In the end, his efforts to catch up with his classmates paid off. He graduated from high school only a few months late.

Around that time, Eddie signed with a talent agent, King Broder. Sometimes the teenager was so eager to get a gig he called clubs and tried to book his act by pretending he was his own agent. One way or another, the bookings came through. He performed at Richard M. Dixon's White House Inn in Massapequa, the Blue Dolphin in Uniondale, the East Side Comedy Club in Huntington, and other Long Island–based clubs. His act consisted of impressions followed by what he called a tribute to Richard Pryor—a half hour of routines based on material from Pryor's comedy albums. In his spare time, Eddie began to try his hand at writing his own material.

Performing at nightclubs meant coming home late every night and sleeping in each morning. Eddie's stepfather refused to consider these comedy stints real jobs; he wanted Eddie to understand the meaning of work and kept after him to get up early and look for a job. Eddie did get up—only to go to his friend Clint Smith's house to catch up on his sleep. Running out of patience, Vernon, Sr., took Eddie to a local mall and insisted he look for work. Eddie landed a job at a Chandler's shoe store.

Meanwhile, Lillian badgered Eddie to enroll at Nassau Community College in Garden City, New York. She believed that he needed a college education in case his career as a comedian did not pan out.

To please his mother, he enrolled at the school in the fall of 1980 and declared theater as his major.

About three weeks after classes began, Eddie's friend Bob Nelson put in a word for him with the owners of the Comic Strip in Manhattan. His nightclub appearance there was a success, and it effectively ended the 19-year-old's academic career. Within a matter of months, he was getting a different kind of education: as a Not Ready for Prime Time Player on "Saturday Night Live."

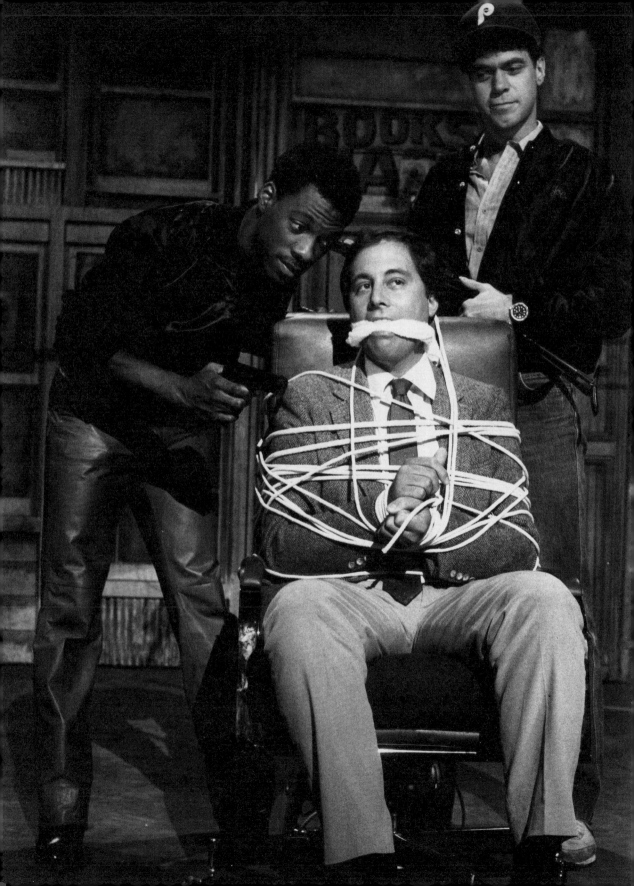

3

"LIVE, FROM NEW YORK!"

—————— ❦ ——————

Murphy and Joe Piscopo (right) threaten a bound-and-gagged Brandon Tartikoff, NBC's head of programming, in a "Saturday Night Live" skit. In the early 1980s, Murphy and Piscopo were the show's two most popular performers.

MAKING EDDIE MURPHY a full-fledged member of "Saturday Night Live" certainly helped the show as it floundered through its first season with a new cast. Still, many problems arose among the program's producer, writers, and performers. Murphy and fellow cast member Joe Piscopo tried to distance themselves from these problems as much as possible.

The difficulties came to a head—and an end—in late February 1981, when one of the show's actors accidentally uttered an obscenity on the show. A short time later, Jean Doumanian was fired, and another producer, Dick Ebersol, was brought in to replace her.

When Ebersol came on board in March, he did a thorough job of housecleaning. Most of the cast and several writers were fired. Murphy and Piscopo were among the few who kept their jobs.

Two shows later, "Saturday Night Live," with its new cast in place, was reviewed by the critics and was once again declared "watchable." But the 1980–81 season was cut short when the show's writers became involved in a contract dispute with NBC and went on strike. Lacking the writers to produce new material, "Saturday Night Live" was put on hold until after the contract matter was cleared up. The delay proved to be a godsend—it gave the new staff time to make improvements to the show, out of the public's watchful eye.

Ebersol made it clear at the beginning of the 1981–82 season that Murphy and Piscopo were his favorite performers among the Not Ready for Prime Time Players. Accordingly, the two comedians received more air time than anyone else in the cast. Murphy made the most of this opportunity, unleashing an arsenal of memorable characters that would make him a favorite with viewers across the nation.

In his second season on "Saturday Night Live," Murphy introduced the character of Little Richard Simmons, who was a strange cross between rock-and-roll singer Little Richard and exercise guru Richard Simmons. Decked out in a Little Richard–style wig and a warm-up suit favored by Simmons, Murphy cut loose with a parody of the rock and roller's signature song, "Good Golly Miss Molly." A group of overweight women clad in leotards shared the stage with him and exercised as he chirped, "Good golly Miss Molly, you look like a hog! Well, you better start running 'cause it's much too late to jog."

Murphy subsequently appeared on the show as Tyrone Green, a convict and a poet. In a segment titled "Prose and Cons," he was shown behind prison bars, reciting the poem "Kill My Landlord." The verse ended with the lines: "Got no reason/ What the heck/ Kill my landlord/ C-I-L-L my landlord." The character's inability to spell the word *kill* made a mockery of pretentious poets.

Another character whom Murphy introduced was Buckwheat, a grown-up version of the pickaninny seen on the 1950s television show "The Little Rascals." The Buckwheat character had taken shape in Murphy's mind during his stand-up days on Long Island, after he had tired of his Richard Pryor tribute and had begun to write his own material.

Portraying a grown-up version of "The Little Rascals" character Buckwheat, Murphy performs a "Saturday Night Live" sketch with another of the Not Ready for Prime Time Players, Mary Gross.

"I'd start riffing with the audience, looking for new material," Murphy recalled. "One night I got to talking about the Little Rascals and I said, 'I'm from a predominantly black family, and I have yet to meet a brother named Buckwheat. I can just see him. 'How ya doin'? My name's Buckwheat. Most people are named after their father. Well, I was named after my father's favorite breakfast cereal.' The audience loved it, so I just kept going. I said, 'Yeah, I got a sister named Shredded Wheat. And I have a retarded brother named Special K.' "

Murphy's characterization proved to be controversial, however. Some black comedians felt that his Buckwheat, who mangled the English language so badly he was hard to comprehend, depicted their race in an unflattering light.

"I do Buckwheat," Murphy responded, "because I think it's funny, and the character is too absurd, abstract and ridiculous to be taken seriously. White people don't look at Buckwheat and say, 'Yes, that's the way blacks dress and act.' "

Another Murphy character who rankled some people was Velvet Jones, a slick television huckster who sells books of questionable value. By imitating low-budget television commercials in which the maker of a product sells the item himself, Murphy meant for Velvet Jones to be a spoof.

Like Buckwheat, Velvet Jones was a character designed to highlight stereotypical beliefs about blacks. And to some blacks, seeing black characters portrayed as slow or illiterate was no laughing matter. When some observers criticized Murphy for playing the part of a pimp, he defended the Velvet Jones character. "Velvet is *not* a pimp, he's a hustler," Murphy said. "If blacks take it wrong, too bad." Whites, in fact, were just as often the butt of Murphy's jokes on "Saturday Night Live." He usually poked fun at whites by portraying them as uptight, rigid, and unnecessarily fearful of blacks.

Murphy delights one of his favorite performers, Stevie Wonder, with a masterful imitation of the singer during a "Saturday Night Live" skit. According to Dick Ebersol, the show's producer, Murphy "is a much better observer of people of anyone I know. . . . He watches people and drains from them and takes it into himself."

For the most part, Murphy did not try to be political in his humor. He felt that his primary job was to entertain. He has since maintained that people want to have a good time without being hit with a heavy message. Still, he has managed to get political messages across numerous times, in subtle and not-so-subtle ways.

One of Murphy's most popular characters on "Saturday Night Live" was Mr. Robinson, a takeoff of the genteel host of the children's television show "Mr. Rogers' Neighborhood." Murphy opened the segment with a parody of Mr. Rogers's opening song, although the lyrics that Mr. Robinson sang were obviously directed at white viewers: "I hope to get to move into your neighborhood someday/Problem is, when I move in, y'all move away."

In addition to the numerous memorable characters Murphy created on "Saturday Night Live," he proved to be a master impersonator, doing uncannily accurate impressions of singers James Brown and Michael Jackson, an aging Muhammad Ali, and a cigar-smoking Bill Cosby. Murphy, impersonating Stevie Wonder, teamed up with Joe Piscopo, playing the part of Frank Sinatra, to create skits that were as brilliant as they were funny. In one sketch, "Frank" and "Stevie" got together to sing their own version of the Stevie Wonder–Paul McCartney hit "Ebony and Ivory." "I am dark and you are light," Murphy sang, perfectly imitating Wonder's voice and head-lolling mannerisms. "You are blind as a bat and I have sight," Piscopo crooned back.

Some people objected to Murphy's role in the skit, saying it was cruel to make fun of a blind man. Yet the real Stevie Wonder had listened to the show and had loved the skit because it did not treat him differently from other people. "I think it's very beautiful actually," the recording star told *Jet* magazine. "I have been very impressed with what comedians have

Director Walter Hill (center) picked a winning combination when he chose Murphy to costar with actor Nick Nolte (left) in the 1982 film 48 HRS. *The movie proved to be so popular that Murphy and Nolte were asked to reprise their roles seven years later in* Another 48 HRS.

done in terms of bridging the gap" between the physically challenged and the rest of society.

No matter what controversy Murphy's characters or impersonations stirred up, the fact remained that in his second season on "Saturday Night Live" he was one of the show's main attractions. No longer could he walk down the street without fans shouting, "Hey, Eddie!" And he was keenly aware that he was on the verge of making it big. "If I don't die in a plane crash or something, this country has a rare opportunity to watch a great talent grow," he told *TV Guide* in mid-1982. "I'll do one more year on this show, then branch out. I could leave now, do a string of B movies and be rich. But I want it to be right, be *perfect*. Pryor. The Beatles. I want to be the Beatles of comedy."

Murphy did not have to wait long before branching out. Hollywood was soon knocking on his door. Among his admirers was film director Walter Hill, who was looking for an actor to play the part of Reggie Hammond in *48 HRS*, an action thriller that was slated to star Nick Nolte. Word had it that Murphy's idol, Richard Pryor, had turned down the role. After watching videotapes of Murphy on "Saturday Night Live," Hill sent a copy of the script to the young comedian, who quickly agreed to play the part of the suave, fast-talking convict whom Nolte enlists to hunt down a murderer.

After working with Murphy, Nolte stated that his costar's talent speaks for itself. "I know everybody is saying that I helped him or taught him, but no, that's just Eddie's acting ability," Nolte said. "We just liked each other and the chemistry worked." Hill had nothing but praise for Murphy, too. "The advantage with Eddie is you accept him as Reggie," the director said. "It's not just a gifted comedian doing a star turn. He's got such a strong center, a strong feeling of who

In Murphy's first feature film, 48 HRS., he played the character of Reggie Hammond, a fast-talking convict who is enlisted to help a hard-boiled cop, played by Nick Nolte (left).

he is . . . he's remarkable." For his part, Murphy thanked each man for "taking me under his wing."

Released in late 1982, *48 HRS* was an immediate hit, grossing $5 million in the first week. The film went on to earn about $100 million, making it a smashing success and propelling Murphy into movie stardom. Following the release of *48 HRS*, Paramount, the studio that had produced the film, signed

him to a $1 million deal, thereby guaranteeing that he would continue to make movies with their company. Murphy proudly displayed an enlarged copy of the check on the 17th floor of 30 Rockefeller Plaza. And with that, the comedy star fulfilled a prophecy he had made back in high school: that he would be famous by the time he was 19 years old and a millionaire by age 22. ❧

4

BRANCHING OUT

At a New York City record store, Murphy poses in front of posters advertising the release of his second comedy album, Eddie Murphy: Comedian, *in 1983. Like his first release,* Eddie Murphy, *it received a Grammy Award nomination for Best Comedy Album.*

FOLLOWING THE SUCCESS of Eddie Murphy's first movie, people began to wonder whether he would return to "Saturday Night Live" for another season. He did not particularly want to continue on the show, but Dick Ebersol was not ready to let him go. The producer told the 22-year-old star that "Saturday Night Live" would probably be canceled if he did not return to the program.

In the end, Murphy gave in to Ebersol, but not before he had negotiated a special deal. Murphy would be paid $300,000 to perform live in half of the season's 20 shows, and he was allowed to tape a number of sketches that would be aired in the remaining programs. The latter part of the agreement marked a first for the show because up to that point, the entire show had always been aired live.

NBC immediately renewed "Saturday Night Live" as soon as Murphy signed on. Yet Murphy himself regretted his decision to return almost the moment he made it. His two favorite writers, Barry Blaustein and David Sheffield, had left the "Saturday Night Live" team to write screenplays in Hollywood, and most of the new material that was being penned for him made him unhappy. He felt that the mediocre material posed a risk to his career. Nevertheless, the

Playing the part of con artist Billy Ray Valentine, Murphy tries to hustle a tycoon, played by actor Don Ameche, in the 1983 movie Trading Places. *Murphy's second film, it offered a satiric look at greed in America.*

young comedian fulfilled his obligation to the show, all the while counting the weeks until he was released from the program. On February 25, 1984, he said good-bye to "Saturday Night Live" for good.

At the time, Murphy felt relieved to be moving on. His attitude toward his departure changed some years later, however, as he looked back on his days of writing for and performing on live television. "When I left in 1984, I told every journalist I hated the show," he said in a 1990 interview. "But in retrospect, it was the most fun I ever had. I loved working with Joe [Piscopo] and Tim [Kazurinsky]. I loved constantly being under the gun and having to write all the time."

All told, "Saturday Night Live" was an important part of Murphy's career. For one thing, he did some of his best work while he was on the program, receiving two Emmy Award nominations for his performances and sharing a nomination for his writing contributions. And it was through "Saturday Night Live" that America discovered the comic genius of Eddie Murphy.

Meanwhile, Murphy had been working double time. He had started out as a stand-up comedian, and he did not entirely abandon performing onstage after achieving Hollywood stardom. He continued to make live concert appearances, which in turn led to the making of two comedy albums and two taped performances that were as successful as they were controversial.

Murphy's first comedy album, *Eddie Murphy*, came along when he was very young and very hot. It was made in 1982, at a time when he had just received critical acclaim for his "Saturday Night Live" performances and had just signed on to film *48 HRS.* Not one to rest on his laurels, he returned to the Comic Strip in New York City and recorded his stand-up act in front of a live audience.

As it turned out, making *Eddie Murphy* was well worth the effort. The album was a hit with his fans. It also received a Grammy Award nomination for Best Comedy Album and Best R&B Instrumental Performance for the album's single, "Boogie in Your Butt."

The following year, Murphy took his stand-up act on the road and embarked on a nationwide tour. His second album, *Eddie Murphy: Comedian*, was recorded live during his performance at Constitution Hall in Washington, D.C. The album went gold—it produced more than $1 million in sales—and was also nominated for a Grammy Award for Best Comedy Album.

But not only was this album nominated—it won. Murphy thus received a Grammy Award—the highest honor bestowed on a recording star—when he was only 22 years old. The occasion was a source of great pride to him. After the awards ceremony, he took the miniature gramophone to his parents' home in Roosevelt, handed it to them, and said, "Well, I never won a trophy as a kid. . . ."

Between the time of the release of *48 HRS* and Murphy's Grammy Award, Paramount signed him to costar with actress Jamie Lee Curtis and fellow "Saturday Night Live" alumnus Dan Aykroyd in *Trading Places*. "I signed to do *Trading Places*," he said, "even before I saw *48 HRS* on screen."

Like *48 HRS*, the fast-paced *Trading Places* was a perfect showcase for Murphy's skills as a comic actor. In the movie, he played the part of Billy Ray Valentine, a street hustler and con artist who becomes a commodities broker when two wealthy brothers, played by Don Ameche and Ralph Bellamy, wage a bet to find out if a person's character is shaped by heredity or environment. The brothers arrange to switch Valentine's situation in life with that of one of their wealthy employees, Louis Winthorpe III, played by Dan Aykroyd. But by the movie's end, Valentine and Winthorpe have banded together to turn the tables on the two brothers.

The film, released in the summer of 1983, was a runaway hit. The critics heaped praise on Murphy for his performance in *Trading Places*. "Eddie is a force to be reckoned with," reported *Time* magazine. "Murphy is the most dynamic new comic talent around, a quicksilver quick-change artist whose rapport with the audience is instantaneous," added *Newsweek*. John Landis, who had directed Murphy in the film, said, "He's probably the most naturally talented actor

I've ever worked with. Everyone says he's a great stand-up comic, but truthfully, I don't think that's his area of brilliance at all." Landis then compared Murphy with two great comic actors: "I think Eddie's Peter Sellers, Alec Guinness." To top off the accolades, Murphy was awarded the 1983 Image Award for Best Actor in a Motion Picture by the National Association for the Advancement of Colored People (NAACP) and was nominated for a Golden Globe Award by the Hollywood Foreign Press Association.

By now, with two highly successful movies to Murphy's credit, Paramount was anxious to keep the hottest comic actor in America within the fold. Accordingly, the studio signed him to an exclusive $15 million, five-picture contract that also included a percentage of the profits from his films. The agreement was said to contain "the biggest personal service deal in movie history." In addition, Murphy received

Murphy shakes hands with Paramount Pictures chairman Frank Mancuso after cementing a multipicture deal with the studio in 1984.

Murphy had a cameo role as a befuddled U.S. Army technician testing the Annihilator tank in Best Defense, *a 1984 film starring Dudley Moore (center). It was the first movie Murphy appeared in to fare poorly at the box office.*

a $4 million cash bonus just for signing the contract—a first in Hollywood history.

And the compensation did not stop there. The studio also agreed to finance the newly created Eddie Murphy Productions. While the purpose of this Los Angeles–based company was to develop and produce new films, Murphy did not have to star in all of them; he was free to choose his projects. At the age of 22, he had become a major power broker in Hollywood. Eddie Murphy, it seemed, could do no wrong.

Then came *Best Defense.* Eager to capitalize on Murphy's popularity, Paramount executives reportedly offered him $1 million to play a cameo role in the picture, which starred comedian Dudley Moore. The offer meant only two weeks of work, and the paycheck was hard to resist. Murphy agreed to take the part, but he later came to regret his decision, for the movie was a flop.

In his role as "strategic guest star," Murphy played the part of an army technician who tries to teach American allies how to use a state-of-the-art tank designed by Dudley Moore's character. The script was so bad that even two actors of Murphy's and Moore's caliber could not save it. "The prospect of Dudley Moore and Eddie Murphy teaming their comic talents tantalizes the mind," *Newsweek* said of the film. "By the time the bullets start to fly . . . one knows all too well what this movie is: grindingly unfunny."

Murphy has since pointed out that *Best Defense* is the only movie he has ever agreed to make against his better instincts. He has also noted that, much to his dismay, the film was billed as an "Eddie Murphy picture" even though he played only a small part in it.

After *Best Defense* crashed resoundingly at the box office, some critics wondered if Murphy was a flash in the pan. But those who doubted whether the young comedian from Roosevelt, Long Island, would enjoy a long run as a major film star would soon learn that he was going to be a presence in the movie industry for a long time to come. ❦

5

"MR. BOX OFFICE"

No ONE QUITE remembers who first thought of casting Eddie Murphy in *Beverly Hills Cop*. The movie, a pet project at Paramount, had been kicking around the studio for years. Several screenplay treatments had been written for *Beverly Hills Cop*, but the project had languished. Then the script was dusted off once again and offered to Sylvester Stallone and Mickey Rourke; for various reasons, both actors declined. Meanwhile, Paramount executives were anxiously looking for another film for Murphy to make. When the script for *Beverly Hills Cop* finally landed in his hands, he knew within 24 hours that he wanted it to be his next project.

Beverly Hills Cop opened on December 5, 1984, and it immediately became obvious that Murphy had made the right choice. In the first three weeks of its release, the movie brought in an astounding $64 million. It ultimately grossed $235 million.

Beverly Hills Cop marked a key point in Murphy's career because it was the first movie in which he received star billing. In his previous pictures, he had been teamed with an actor who possessed proven box-office appeal. This time, it was up to Murphy alone to draw audiences, and he did. *Beverly Hills Cop* became the seventh-highest-grossing picture of all time.

In January 1985, with people all across the country lining up at theaters to see *Beverly Hills Cop*, *Newsweek* featured the 23-year-old star on its cover, proclaiming him "Mr. Box Office." There were more accolades to follow. In the People's Choice Award

Murphy's rollicking portrayal of policeman Axel Foley in Beverly Hills Cop, the first film in which he received top billing, helped the actor-comedian acquire a major title, Mr. Box Office. This 1984 release became one of the top grossing comedies in motion picture history.

competition, *Beverly Hills Cop* was named Favorite Motion Picture, and Murphy was co-named Favorite All-Around Entertainer. He also received a Best Actor nomination for a Golden Globe Award and was named Star of the Year at the 1985 ShoWest Convention of Motion Picture Exhibitors.

It is no wonder, then, that Martin Brest, who directed Murphy in *Beverly Hills Cop*, said of him, "He's a comic genius." In his portrayal of Axel Foley, a street-smart Detroit cop who goes to Beverly Hills to track down his best friend's killer, Murphy was witty, charming, and always entertaining. Judge Reinhold, who played the part of cop Billy Rosewood in the film, said of its star, "I kept looking for Eddie's tragic flaw, but I couldn't find it. He's a gifted, comedic Mozart."

Murphy poses with his number one fan: his mother, Lillian.

Murphy's spontaneous contributions to the film's script often left screenwriter Daniel Petrie, Jr., and director Brest dazzled. In the film's opening sequence, Foley, who is working undercover to bust a cigarette-smuggling ring in Detroit, breaks into a "bravura parody of street jive," said one critic in describing Murphy's performance. In another scene, in which Murphy's casually dressed character arrives at a posh Hollywood hotel, the quick-thinking Foley manages to talk his way into being given a complimentary suite at the Beverly Palm Hotel by posing as a journalist for *Rolling Stone* in hot pursuit of Michael Jackson.

Perhaps the most spirited scene of *Beverly Hills Cop* is the one in which the script called for Foley to bluff his way into a restaurant at an exclusive men's club, where his nemesis and his henchman are having lunch. Brest had considered several scenarios that would get Foley into the club, but none worked. Finally, the director approached Murphy and explained the problem. The actor bowed his head to think; within minutes, he had the solution.

In the film, viewers see Murphy assume the character of lispy-voiced Ramón, who swishes past the restaurant's maître d' while saying that he has to deliver his lunching lover an embarrassing message: that he has herpes. "It couldn't have taken him more than four seconds and he proceeded to spill out the whole scene," recalled Brest. "I fell on the floor laughing. He put his makeup on, we walked over to the set, and he did it."

So resounding was the success of *Beverly Hills Cop* that Murphy's contract with Paramount was renegotiated. It turned into a $25-million deal for five pictures plus a major concert film.

Murphy's popularity at the box office allowed him to enjoy a life-style known to few, especially at such a young age. After his breakthrough on "Saturday Night Live," he had moved into his own apartment, and later a house, in Freeport, Long Island. "I have to be close to Mommy," he said at the time.

But in 1985, following the success of his first three films, Murphy, then 24, bought a $4.5 million colonial red-brick mansion, complete with stately white columns gracing each side of the main entrance. The house, located in Englewood Cliffs, New Jersey, was only a short distance from Manhattan via the George Washington Bridge. He subsequently bought another house only five minutes away for his mother and stepfather, with whom he remains close.

Shortly after Murphy moved to New Jersey, some of his pals, among them cousin Ray Murphy, Jr., and childhood friend Kenneth Frith—both of whom have worked with the comedian over the years—moved into the mansion with him for a while. Eddie dubbed his new home Bubble Hill. (*Bubble* means "party" in street jargon.) These two words are also etched in stone on the massive wall that surrounds the house. "I built the wall because I felt there was supposed to be a wall there," he said. "It's like going to a premiere in a limousine as opposed to going in a jeep. It's part of that show business bull. . . . You're supposed to have walls; if I had a chainlink fence, it would look weird." The mansion is also protected by wrought-iron electronic portals.

Bubble Hill has more than 22 rooms, including eight bedrooms, eight full bathrooms, two half baths, four fireplaces, and a garage big enough to hold five cars. The four-acre estate was unfinished when Eddie bought it. His mother has since spent a good portion of her time decorating the mansion and supervising construction of a new wing and other amenities.

On entering, guests walk into an exquisite marble foyer. Off the entryway is a formal, conservatively furnished room that serves as Murphy's office for his film and television production companies. Also on the first floor is a large, modern kitchen, a formal

Always one to maintain close ties with his family, Murphy is surrounded (from left to right) by his stepfather, Vernon Lynch; his mother, Lillian; and his half brother, Vernon, Jr. The comedy star also has an older brother, Charles.

dining room, a library, and an elegant living room. Hanging over the mantel in the living room is a painted portrait of Eddie Murphy, and next to it is a framed vest once owned by rock star Jimi Hendrix. Murphy reportedly bought the vest at an auction for $7,150.

The home contains other celebrity memorabilia as well, including items that relate to Elvis Presley. At one time, it was reported that a huge portrait of Presley hung on one of the walls in Murphy's bedroom. In any event, comparisons have been made between Murphy's home and Graceland, Presley's mansion in Memphis, Tennessee.

In addition to the living quarters, Bubble Hill contains everything Murphy needs to enjoy life out of the public eye. A glass-enclosed swimming pool with a large cabana contains a white piano and a Ping-Pong table. Framed magazine covers featuring Murphy line the walls, alongside photos of him with such celebrities as movie star Sylvester Stallone, rock singer David Bowie, boxer Sugar Ray Leonard, and the late entertainer Sammy Davis, Jr.

Murphy's estate also has a state-of-the-art recording studio so he can work on his albums at home. For entertainment, there is a movie screening room, pool room, pinball game room, bowling alley, and fog machine for the dance floor. On the wall of the bowling alley is a mural depicting his family and friends. A fully equipped gym and indoor racquetball court is available for him to work out whenever he pleases. Outside the house is a patio with a barbecue grill and enough chairs for several dozen people, and a basketball court, which sometimes serves as a parking lot for his friends and relatives, who pay frequent visits.

But all was not paradise for Murphy in his sumptuous home. In spite of his immense popularity and luxurious life-style, he was still being criticized in some quarters for his use of profanity in his stage act. "Stand-up is my release, my way of doing whatever I want," he told *Parade* magazine in 1985. "Some people like it, although my movie fans might think it's a little vulgar." Among the critics were his older fans, including Lucille Ball and Bill Cosby, both of whom spoke out against his use of profanity.

The criticism of Murphy's language was nothing, however, compared to the reaction that followed in October 1983, when one of his performances was aired on television as an HBO "On Location" special and was released a month later on videocassette. In this performance, entitled *Delirious*, Murphy cracked jokes about everyone from homosexuals to women. Many people, especially women and members of the gay community, were outraged by these jokes, which they considered narrow-minded attacks.

Murphy meant for his jokes and parodies to be taken lightly, not as serious commentary. Still, he was disturbed by the reaction to *Delirious*. He subsequently apologized to those people whom he had offended, particularly gays and lesbians. "I'm just trying to get a laugh," he explained. "I'm not a hateful person. I get on stage because I like to see people laugh. I don't have to go on tour. I could just do

Wielding a sacred dagger, Murphy attempts to rescue the title character (played by J. L. Reate) from evil forces in the 1986 movie The Golden Child.

movies. But I like to see people smile. I don't want to hurt them."

It was those sentiments, perhaps, that influenced Murphy most when he chose his next film role. After the release of *Beverly Hills Cop*, he considered appearing in *Star Trek IV: The Voyage Home*. "I've always wanted to do *Star Trek*," he said. "I'm a Trekkie. . . . The script was developed, but it didn't quite work out, so we dropped the idea. It was a choice between *Star Trek IV* and *The Golden Child*, and I chose *The Golden Child* because I thought it would be better for my career." Eager to play a more serious character than he had in his past films, Murphy also felt that as a black actor, he should not always be cast in roles that required him to play the part of a gun-toting cop or a convict on the run.

The Golden Child was released in December 1986 and combined fantasy with the supernatural. Murphy played the part of Chandler Jarrell, whose occupation is finding missing children and whose mission in the film is to rescue a youth called the Golden Child, who has been kidnapped by evil forces. Murphy performed well, but the movie received mixed reviews, with some critics saying that the comedic touches in the film seemed forced.

The Golden Child was considered something of a disappointment, even though it grossed $100 million—a huge success by box-office standards. The movie did not do as well as Murphy's previous blockbuster, *Beverly Hills Cop*, and because Murphy's star had risen so high so fast, enormous expectations had been heaped on his shoulders.

"In retrospect, I might have been better off doing *Star Trek*," Murphy said. "*Golden Child* started out as a good picture. I don't think it's a bad movie. I think there are some bad things in it. I don't think it was done properly or looked quite right. I don't think *Golden Child* was what it could have been. I picked it because I wanted something where I wasn't shooting guns."

For his next film, Murphy returned to familiar ground; he reprised the role of Axel Foley in *Beverly Hills Cop 2*. In this May 1987 release, Foley returns to Beverly Hills after he hears that a gang of robbers has seriously wounded Andy Bogomil, the lieutenant whom Murphy's character had befriended in the first movie. The action follows Foley as he confronts the upper crust of Beverly Hills, this time to track down the thieves.

In deciding to appear in the film, Murphy again showed that his instincts were on the mark. *Beverly*

Hills Cop 2 earned $250 million worldwide and was the biggest moneymaker of the year. And in recognition of his acting talents, he received an Otto Award from *Bravo*, a leading German magazine. He was also voted Favorite Movie Actor by Nickelodeon, the children's cable television network, and was named Best Male Actor by readers of *Ebony* magazine.

But the greatest testimony to Murphy's star status took place even before filming began on *Beverly Hills Cop 2*. The movie was originally slated to be called *London Cop*, but Murphy did not want to spend an extended period of time in Great Britain. So the film was set once again in Beverly Hills. The decision to shift the making of the movie to California indicated the power Murphy could wield. At age 26, he remained Hollywood's hottest star.

6

"THERE'S THIS BIG MISCONCEPTION . . ."

EDDIE MURPHY HAD been developing a reputation in the media for years as a partying guy who loved leather, jewelry, and fast cars. Murphy, they said, would visit nightclubs regularly to pick up women, and he would not go anywhere without a large entourage in tow. In addition, he was accused of becoming isolated from the world, living behind the sheltering walls of his New Jersey mansion, surrounded by an ever-present group of flatterers and cronies.

But were any of these press accounts really true? Who is the real Eddie Murphy?

On the question of his relationships with women, Murphy told *People* magazine in 1988, "When I first got in the public eye, when I was like 19, 20, 21, I raised much hell." But he outgrew that urge fairly quickly, and his social life soon tamed down. By 1985, he was engaged to Lisa Figueroa, who at the time was a biology major at Adelphi University on Long Island. "I'm not a swinger like I used to be," he said in discussing his relationship with Figueroa.

Their engagement, however, ended after about a year. "We just outgrew each other," Murphy explained. "We were too young to be talking about marriage." At the time of his engagement, he was 24 years old.

Even though Murphy was still young and eligible and countless women would have welcomed the chance to go out with him, he did not return to his

Murphy becomes the 171st Hollywood star to have his handprints and footprints preserved in cement outside Mann's Chinese Theater in Los Angeles. The ceremony was held on May 14, 1987, three days before Beverly Hills Cop 2 *premiered at the theater.*

carefree ways after the breakup. Still, his reputation as a womanizer remained stubbornly intact. "The perception that people have of me as Eddie with the leather suit on and chicks and bodyguards and all that stuff, that's something from a nine-year-old image," he told the *New York Times* in 1992. "That's from back when I did *Raw* and *Delirious*. I haven't been that guy in almost ten years, and people still think of me as that image."

Perhaps part of the reason the image has persisted is that over the years Murphy has become increasingly reluctant to grant interviews to the press. Although he was once fairly open with journalists, willingly sharing his views and giving them tours of his home, that all changed in 1987, when a profile of him appeared in *Interview* magazine. "The guy came to my house, and he was the nicest guy in the world," Murphy said of the reporter who wrote the piece, "and he tore me up."

Whenever Murphy does speak to the press, he maintains that he is an average, normal person like anyone else. "I have very normal thoughts," he told one interviewer. "There's nothing I've ever done that I'm ashamed of. There's nothing that I regret doing. I'm one of the straightest people I know."

If Murphy continues to have problems with the press, it is because, he says, "I'm not very humble in their eyes." He points out, though, that "what made me successful was my boldness. That's part of my humor. That's part of my character."

Murphy realizes that the parts he has played on film and the routines he has performed doing stand-up comedy could have contributed to some of the misconceptions about him. "People expect me to be this arrogant jerk when they meet me," he said. "That's just my stage personality. . . . Offstage, I'm not hard and nasty and unfeeling. I believe in God—

Murphy returns to stand-up comedy in his second concert film, Raw, *which was shot during two 1987 performances he gave in New York City.*

strongly. I get hurt over women leaving me, just like everybody else."

And, just like everybody else, Murphy has had his share of problems. "There's this big misconception about being famous and rich," he observed. "The misconception is that once you're rich, you're straight. But you can have financial problems and everything else, only on a much grander scale." Indeed, he has a payroll of some 50 people, many of whom often come to him with *their* problems. "Everybody tries to get close to you, and [there's] the weight of being the patriarch in your family. It's just a bunch of stuff."

Loyal to a fault, Murphy has had several close friends and family members work with him on his films and for his television and movie production companies. "You have four or five friends in a lifetime," Murphy has observed. "My true friends—the guys I hung out with when I was in junior high school and high school—work for me." Kenneth Frith and Ray Murphy, Jr., Eddie's cousin, are both executives with Murphy's film production company; the latter also served as the associate producer of *Boomerang*. And Clint Smith, Murphy's best friend from high school, has served as vice-president of Eddie Murphy Television Enterprises, formed in 1988 with Paramount Television and CBS-TV.

"The people that are related to me," Murphy has said, "are as competent or more competent than anybody else that I'm going to work with and I know have my best interests at heart." In fact, it has been his long-standing policy that if a family member or close friend shows an interest in any area of production, he or she is given an opportunity to learn it. His older brother, Charlie, for instance, has been part of Murphy's management team, and his stepfather helped promote his 1987 *Raw* concert tour. Charlie and younger brother, Vernon, Jr., own Murphy's merchandising company, which sells T-shirts, posters, and other items at Eddie's concerts.

As Murphy said in a 1987 *Jet* interview, "I could just write my family a check every week and they don't do anything. But it would be a sin because they're such productive people. . . . They're hard workers and my best interest is what's important to them."

Murphy is also known to take an interest in people who have less than his own family members do. A few years back, he was known to drive around Manhattan's drug-infested streets and lecture addicts about the evils of drug use. "I've sat crackheads down in my car," he recalled, "and talked to them: *'What's wrong with you?* I've talked about their families. . . . I've seen people crying. . . . I hope I can inspire them to do something. . . . But turning their lives around is something they have to do themselves."

Murphy found himself embroiled in his own troubles in 1987, after the release of *Beverly Hills Cop 2,* when he discovered that he could still cause a tremendous uproar. That is exactly what he did with the release of his second concert film, *Raw,* which made the controversy that followed *Delirious* seem tame in comparison. He had gone on a cross-country tour in 1987 with his stand-up act, and *Raw* was filmed during two special concerts at Madison Square Garden's Felt Forum in New York City. The tour came on the heels of his break up with Lisa Figueroa, a paternity suit, and a lawsuit filed against him by his agent, King Broder, who was asking for 25 percent of

Murphy attends the premiere of Beverly Hills Cop *with fiancée, Lisa Figueroa, who helped suppress his taste for the fast life. In fact, by the time they broke off their engagement, he no longer practiced his carefree ways.*

Murphy's income. The 26-year-old comedian could not have been in a worse frame of mind.

Angry and hostile, Murphy centered his performance on scatological jokes about opportunistic women who wanted his money and did not care about him. Needless to say, this did little to endear Murphy to his female fans, who were infuriated by his wholesale characterization of them as greedy, dependent, and manipulative. Murphy also did a routine depicting the macho television personality Mr. T as gay, and he did a spoof on the popular television sitcom characters Ralph Kramden and Ed Norton, the blue-collar husbands in the "The Honeymooners," presenting them as homosexual lovers.

Murphy held nothing back. But in letting all his pent-up emotions pour out, he managed once again to offend women and homosexuals, as well as blacks, who were upset with his sharp-edged imitation of Bill Cosby. Perhaps because of his fantastic success and wealth and his broken engagement, Murphy's view of women had become somewhat mean spirited and distrustful. Many men cheered his jokes, but most women fumed, especially black women, who were insulted by his attitude toward them.

"I did *Raw* at a really bitter stage of my life," Murphy told *People* magazine a year later. "I look at it now and cringe. It's not so much that I think *Raw* wasn't funny, but I can't believe what I was feeling then." A few years later, when the subject of *Raw* came up again, he said, "I regret how hostile I was." Nevertheless, *Raw* proved to be one of the most popular concert films ever made, grossing more than $50 million.

Murphy was hardly the first performer to employ a no-holds-barred attitude during his stand-up performances. In the last few decades, Lenny Bruce, George Carlin, Redd Foxx, and Richard Pryor have headed a long list of comedians who have been controversial in their acts. Onstage, they tackled taboo subjects and used profanity.

There was, however, one subject that remained off-limits to Murphy: religion. "I'm a spiritual person," he explained. "I'd feel welcome in any church, so I wouldn't make jokes about anybody's God."

Following the making of *Raw*, Murphy wanted to stretch his wings and play a role that would erase some of the public's bitter feelings about his brand of humor and that would be entirely different from any part he had previously accepted. Recognizing that none of his characters so far had shown a romantic side, he said that he wanted to do "a light comedy with romance." More important, he wanted to make a movie that would place blacks in a positive light.

Frustrated with the kinds of scripts he was being offered, Murphy came up with the idea for his next movie, *Coming to America*. With a screenplay written by his two favorite writers from "Saturday Night Live," Barry Blaustein and David Sheffield, the film promised to be another big hit.

The ingredients were all there: Murphy was cast as Prince Akeem, the only child of the King and Queen (played, respectively, by James Earl Jones and Madge Sinclair) of the mythical African principality of Zamunda. The story line of the movie is that Prince Akeem has just come of age, and his royal parents are arranging for him to marry. But the pampered prince does not like the idea of marrying a woman he has never even met. In interviews, Murphy noted that some loose parallels could be drawn to his own life at the time. "I think everybody who doesn't have somebody," he said, "is looking for someone to call their own, even though they might say they *want* to be single."

In the movie, the prince convinces his father to let him go with his sidekick, Semmi (played by Murphy's close friend Arsenio Hall), to America, ostensibly to "sow his wild oats." But in making his request, Akeem has something better in mind. He and Semmi decide to travel to the borough of Queens in New York City. They reason, what better place to find a queen?

The movie, released in June 1988, showed an extremely charming side of the Eddie Murphy persona: sensitive, vulnerable, and looking for a woman who would love him for being himself. Among the other highlights of *Coming to America* are the scenes in which Murphy and Hall play characters other than Akeem and Semmi. Wearing layers of makeup, Murphy appears, for example, as a crotchety old Jewish gentleman and Hall steals one scene as what the credits call an Extremely Ugly Girl.

In spite of the pair's on-screen highjinks, *Coming to America* received mixed reviews. Murphy's fans, however, lined up to see the film, and it took in a phenomenal $350 million at the box office.

More accolades soon followed. In 1988, Murphy received a second Otto Award. He also won the

People's Choice Award for Best Comedy Actor and World Almanac's Top Hero Award. He was named Entertainer of the Year at the NAACP Image Awards, and he was presented with a Tree of Life Award at the Black Oscar Nominees Dinner.

Unfortunately, making *Coming to America* was not a completely positive experience for Murphy. He had initially considered directing the movie himself but decided to let John Landis handle the job. After making *Trading Places*, Landis had fallen on hard times; his last three movies had not done well at the box office, and three actors had lost their lives during the making of *The Twilight Zone: The Movie*, which he had directed. Though Landis, brought to court and accused of negligence on the *Twilight Zone* set, successfully weathered the trial, his career was in trouble.

In handpicking Landis as his director, Murphy believed he was helping out an old friend. But the director reportedly did not see the situation in the same way. Evidently, he was upset that Murphy had not made an appearance at his trial to lend "moral

Displaying his versatility as an actor, Murphy played four different roles in the 1988 film Coming to America: *Prince Akeem of the mythical African principality of Zamunda (opposite page, left); Clarence, a New York City barber (opposite page, right); Saul, an elderly Jewish man (below, left); and entertainer Randy Watson (below, right).*

support," and he was still nursing this "slight." Harsh words were exchanged on the set of *Coming to America*, and a rather tense atmosphere prevailed throughout the filming. Landis later acknowledged that there had been "personality conflicts" on the set.

The second development that made *Coming to America* a less than happy experience was the fact that Paramount was sued by the newspaper columnist and humorist Art Buchwald, who claimed that the movie was based on a three-page story idea he had previously sold to the company. Buchwald's treatment was about an African king who is overthrown as ruler of his country when he travels to America. Murphy, who had received story credit for the screenplay of *Coming to America*, maintained that the idea was his own.

Even though it is not unusual for several different people to claim ownership of story ideas in Hollywood, this particular experience left a bitter taste in Murphy's mouth. "I'm sure Art Buchwald, when he looks at *Coming to America*, goes, like, 'Hey, I didn't write that. . . .' He has to," Murphy said. Yet after four years of legal entanglements, a judge decided that the film was based on Buchwald's outline and awarded him $150,000 in damages. "It's water under the bridge," Murphy subsequently responded, pointing out that "it's an issue between Paramount and Art Buchwald—but I know what I wrote and I know what I did."

While *Coming to America* was packing people in at the theaters, Murphy was in the process of purchasing a four-acre estate in Los Angeles's Benedict Canyon from pop singer Cher for approximately $6.5 million. For a few years, he lived in this West Coast home while construction was being completed on Bubble Hill. The Benedict Canyon estate, which is surrounded by a moat, has six bedrooms, seven and a half baths, a pool, a spa, a gym, and an atrium with

Arsenio Hall (right), Murphy's co-star in Coming to America, *shares his good friend's happiness over winning the People's Choice Award for Best Comedy Actor in a Motion Picture. Murphy received the award in March 1989.*

a skylight. Murphy, however, is a New Yorker at heart, and he considers Bubble Hill his "real" home.

Murphy's decision to settle on the East Coast instead of the West Coast, where most movers and shakers in the movie industry live, offers further testament to his determination to live life on his own terms. Just as noteworthy is Murphy's wish that his family and friends live nearby. "I don't know if it helps me that they're here or not," he has said, "but I love them and want them with me."

Although Bubble Hill has lived up to its name—Murphy has certainly enjoyed good times there—he has long been known as someone who does not experiment with drugs. Nor does he drink or smoke. He never has. "I've never, ever, ever, ever, ever, ever, like, *held* cocaine," he has pointed out. "I'm no advocate of drug use, and I don't [mess] around with anything. No drinking. I hate it."

Certainly the temptations were there. After all, since the age of 15 he had been working stand-up comedy in bars, where liquor flowed freely. Still,

Eddie did not partake. He knew he had something more important to do with his life. Similarly, when he was a teenager and some of his peers were experimenting with drugs, he stood up to group pressure instead of caving in. He once said that if everyone else was doing something, it was cool *not* to do it.

The temptations did not stop once Murphy became a star. One night, when he was still a member of "Saturday Night Live," John Belushi and another comedian took him to a blues bar. "They put [cocaine] on the table and said 'Come on, have a sniff,'" Murphy recalled. "And I really admired these guys—I was nineteen or twenty years old—so I was real close to doing it. But I didn't. I just didn't." By his own account, that night was the closest he ever came to experimenting with drugs. "I was in a circle that was supposed to be hip, and the people I was looking up to in that circle were all doing it." Much to his credit, he had the discipline to go against the crowd instead of doing something just to fit in.

Murphy's strong antidrug stance seems to have won approval from the media. There are other areas of his life, however, in which he and the press do not see eye to eye. "I keep hearing about my 'entourage,'" he has said. In fact, some people in the press have said that the higher Murphy's star has risen, the more he has become like his idol Elvis Presley. In Presley's final years, the idol turned icon lived a life largely sheltered from the public, with only a large cadre of yes-men and hangers-on around for company.

Murphy has refuted this image of himself. "If [actor] Michael J. Fox walks into a restaurant with his friends," he has said, "it's Michael J. Fox and his guests. When Eddie Murphy walks into a room with his friends, it's like, 'Oh, my, it's Eddie Murphy—and his *entourage*.'" To Murphy, there is an underlying racism in such remarks. "I don't *have* an entourage," he has maintained. "I don't have bodyguards. I don't have anybody to, like, choke you and say, 'Get away from this man!' My cousin Ray . . . Kenneth Frith, who we call Fruitie—he went to school with me—and Larry [Johnson]. They're big guys. People see them and it's like, 'Oh. Bodyguards.' "

Although Murphy does not travel with a group of bodyguards, there is always at least one individual who travels with him for security reasons. "I got in a situation about six, seven, years ago," he told *Premiere* magazine in 1992, "where I was by myself and had a fight in a club." The incident, which took place at a Los Angeles nightclub, was reportedly started by a man whose date was looking at Murphy.

Ever since that evening, Murphy has decided that he should not go out alone anymore. Indeed, he is well aware that along with the privileges of being successful come special problems. "All it takes," he says in reference to a celebrity of his stature being badly hurt or even killed, "is one incident."

7

"I JUST WANT TO BE GOOD"

AS EDDIE MURPHY became a major power broker in Hollywood, he found himself being accused by some blacks in the entertainment industry of not doing enough to help other members of his race. In failing to make overtly political films, they said, he was turning his back on blacks. Around the time that *Do the Right Thing* was released in 1989, the film's director, Spike Lee, emerged as one of Murphy's more vocal critics, stating that the former "Saturday Night Live" star was not doing enough to help his people.

"Without me," Murphy said in response to Lee's charge, "I don't think the studios would have put out a movie like *Hollywood Shuffle*, or backed *I'm Gonna Git You Sucka*, or bought *She's Gotta Have It*," three black films that had been released in recent years. Murphy's positive portrayals of blacks on the silver screen and his proven success has paved the way for other blacks to be given an opportunity to make films. "This is why it's weird when a guy like Spike attacks me," Murphy said. "He don't realize that he's around because of the 'Let's get us one, too' attitude." Murphy and Lee have since settled their differences.

And the fact remains that Murphy *has* done a great deal to help blacks. In 1989, he served as honorary chairman of the United Negro College Fund "Parade of Stars" telethon hosted by Lou Rawls. The following year, he announced his chairmanship of the newly organized Paramount/Eddie Murphy Fellowship, a minority outreach program for blacks in the entertainment industry; the fellowship offers employment opportunities in filmmaking and

Appearing on "The Arsenio Hall Show," Murphy causes the talk show host to convulse in laughter. Away from the spotlight, Murphy has said, "You succeed when you accept success, completely and totally."

television at Paramount. He has made numerous sizable donations to black foundations, including the Martin Luther King, Jr., Center for Nonviolent Social Change, and has contributed to such causes as cancer research and the fight against acquired immune deficiency syndrome (AIDS). He rarely discuses his good deeds, which is how he likes it. "It's nobody's business," he maintains.

In 1988, however, Murphy changed his tactic of staying behind the scenes by making a very bold—and very public—statement at the Academy Awards ceremony. He had been selected to present the Oscar for Best Picture of the year—a high honor in itself, for the presentation of the award is the highlight of the evening. In making the presentation, he cracked a few jokes, then his tone became serious.

Murphy took Hollywood's power brokers to task for awarding blacks only three Oscars for acting in the Academy of Arts and Motion Pictures' 60-year history. The first one went to Hattie McDaniel in 1939 for her supporting role in *Gone with the Wind*. Sidney Poitier received the Best Actor award in 1963 for his performance in *Lilies of the Field*. Louis Gossett, Jr., was handed an Oscar in 1983 for his supporting role in *An Officer and a Gentleman*.

"The way it's been going," Murphy remarked, "we get one about every twenty years. So we ain't due for another until about 2004." He concluded his remarks by saying, "I feel that we have to be recognized as a people. . . . Black people will not ride the caboose of society and we will not bring up the rear anymore."

In response to comments that the Academy Awards ceremony was not the proper forum to air such views, Murphy said, "When *do* you accuse the Academy of being racist and be heard—unless you're doing the nominees for the best picture? They're all listening right there. Where am I gonna say it? In *Ebony*? They don't read *Ebony*."

Since the night that Murphy made his speech, two more blacks have been recognized by the Academy for their acting excellence: Denzel Washington, who won the Best Supporting Actor award in 1989 for his role in *Glory*, and Whoopi Goldberg, who was named Best Supporting Actress in 1990 for her part in *Ghost*. A proud Murphy subsequently joked, "I went down first so my brothers could get their trophies!" Just as important, the stand Murphy took silenced his critics and increased his popularity within the black community.

"My dream is just to have black artists appreciated as much as white artists," Murphy observed. "I want us to be able to win Oscars, to do films about our people when we want to, to get films made, to do what we want to as artists. There shouldn't be just Eddie Murphy and Richard Pryor in movies."

To that end, Murphy has been at the forefront in providing opportunities in the film industry for black actors, writers, producers, directors, and other "behind-the-scenes" talent. Scores of blacks were hired to work on- and off-camera in *Coming to America*, for example. John Amos, who had a featured role in the movie, said, "I've been acting twenty-two years, and I've never seen [that] many blacks on a movie set. It's all because of Eddie Murphy. Despite what people might say about him, Eddie's social consciousness speaks for itself."

Murphy's next film after *Coming to America* again enabled him to work with a large number of blacks. It also gave him a chance to do two things he had always wanted to do: direct, and appear in a movie with Richard Pryor. "I had bounced ideas off him lots of times," Murphy said, "but I couldn't come up with the ideal thing." Then, while listening to some of Pryor's old comedy albums, Murphy noted that his idol often portrayed people who frequent the back room of a bar. Murphy thought that perhaps a film based on these characters might appeal to Pryor. He came up with the idea of a movie about two men who own a Harlem gambling club that the Mafia tries to take over. Pryor loved the concept, and *Harlem Nights* was born.

"There hasn't been a film in recent years that has shown Harlem from a black perspective. . . . I wanted to do a film like that," Murphy said. He wrote and produced *Harlem Nights* in addition to directing it. He also appeared in the movie as Pryor's adopted son, Quick. In addition to Pryor, who portrays the owner of the gambling club, the film's all-star cast included Redd Foxx and entertainer Della Reese. As excited

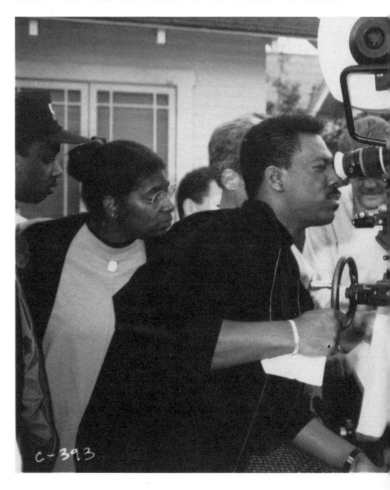

as Murphy was to work with these veteran performers, he also found it somewhat intimidating to direct them, he said later.

For all the promise that *Harlem Nights* showed during its planning stages, the movie proved to be Murphy's first critical flop when it was released in November 1989. The film was attacked for its high level of violence. And when a 17-year-old was shot to death in a movie theater during the film's opening day, some critics said the movie even glorified violence.

Murphy himself admitted that the movie was not as good as it could have been. For one thing, he had

Behind the camera for the first time, Murphy makes his directorial debut in 1989 on the set of Harlem Nights. *He also wrote the screenplay and produced the film.*

Entertainer Della Reese (left) and comedian Redd Foxx (right), who were featured in Harlem Nights, *perform a scene in "The Royal Family." Murphy created and served as executive producer of the critically acclaimed series, which was cut short by Foxx's death.*

written the script in only two weeks. "It was poorly executed, I guess," he said in retrospect. "*Harlem Nights* was a question of wearing too many hats."

Eddie had wanted to try his hand at directing in part because a number of his peers, including Spike Lee and Robert Townsend, were doing it successfully. "I was, like . . . 'I'm the big cat on the block; let me see what it's like to direct,' " Murphy said. But he did not enjoy the experience nearly as much as he had thought he would. "I didn't dig it," he admitted, "and I hated doing it throughout the whole trip, and it affected my performance."

After the debacle of *Harlem Nights*, Murphy was anxious to make a film that would be a surefire crowd pleaser. Recalling the enormous success of *48 HRS*, the first movie he ever made, he agreed to team up again with Nick Nolte and reprise the role of Reggie Hammond in *Another 48 HRS*. Released in June 1990, the movie found its audience—it earned $140 million worldwide—but Murphy acknowledged that the sequel was a weaker version of the original. "The idea was contrived and we threw it together," he said, "and they wrote these big checks out, and we did it."

Murphy was quick to admit the reason behind his agreeing to make a movie that was not up to his usual standards. "That whole thing was out of fear, because *Harlem Nights* was the first time I did a movie that flopped," he said. "I had never gone through that." He added that, after *Beverly Hills Cop*, "everything was going out of control. Everything came too easy. . . . And when the laughs come too easy, you start doing things like walking through movies. You get too comfortable. You start getting out of control. . . . You argue. You get a big head. You wear a leather suit and a glove with a ring on the outside."

The years during and immediately after the making of *Harlem Nights* and *Another 48 HRS* marked a particularly down period for Murphy. He was not getting along with his family; he could not find a good movie to make; and as someone who had always taken pride in his appearance, he had even begun to put on weight. This troubling turn of events, he said, was due to "the pressure trip everybody goes through when you stop being one of the cats and become this *thing*."

A close look at his performance in *Another 48 HRS* was enough to convince Murphy that it was high time for a break. "There's nothing like going into a movie theatre," he recalled, "and looking up on a screen and you're a fat guy in a bad movie." And so the release of *Another 48 HRS* marked the end of a long decade that had produced major changes in Murphy's life, a decade in which the performer had evolved from an up-and-coming comedian into a major film star and a decade in which Murphy's films collectively grossed more than $1 billion worldwide.

Murphy's creative output had been enormous. He had made a movie nearly every year since 1982. He had continued to give stand-up concerts. And he had cut comedy albums as well as all-music recordings.

In addition to his hard work, outside pressures from various lawsuits that had been filed over the past few years proved to be draining. Besides Art Buchwald's lawsuit over *Coming to America*, King Broder, Murphy's manager during his days as a stand-up comic on Long Island, had sued him and had won a reported $1.1 million settlement. Michele Michael, an actress who had been slated to play the female lead in *Harlem Nights*, had sued him for sexual harassment after she was fired from the job. That lawsuit, according to Murphy's manager, Mark Lipsky, was "a major misunderstanding that's been since worked out."

To top off Murphy's troubles, at least three women said they had given birth to his baby. "One woman," noted Lipsky, even "claimed that she was Eddie's wife and sent us her bills to pay." Murphy, who had never been married, responded to the claims of having several children by saying, "Those are [National] Enquirer babies."

But on November 18, 1989, Eddie Murphy acknowledged that he was a father. His daughter, Bria Liana, was born to his steady girlfriend, 24-year-old model Nicole R. Mitchell. In the years that have followed, Murphy and Mitchell have continued to enjoy a committed relationship. They became engaged over Christmas, 1991, and a wedding date was set for March 18, 1993. Meanwhile, the couple had a second child—a boy, Miles Mitchell Murphy, born November, 1992.

How is it that Mitchell won Murphy's heart when others failed? "Nicole is the sweetest person I've ever met, and she doesn't suffocate me," he said. "Women

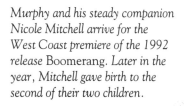

Murphy and his steady companion Nicole Mitchell arrive for the West Coast premiere of the 1992 release Boomerang. *Later in the year, Mitchell gave birth to the second of their two children.*

I've been with tend to get caught up in my life; they don't have their own thing, they wait around for something to happen. Nicole has her own thing *and* she's fine—makes me puff my chest all out when I'm with her. It's very rare that you meet a woman as fine as she is who also has a sense of humor."

These days, Murphy seems more comfortable with the idea of settling down. Not only that, but he appears to have come to terms with his fame and to have made peace with himself and his place in the world. Perhaps most important, through his relationship with his daughter and son, he has found happiness in his personal life—something that no amount of money can buy.

Murphy's fresh outlook may be due in part to his turning 30 years old. In April 1991, to celebrate the event, he took about a half-dozen friends and relatives on an impromptu trip to Half Moon Bay in Jamaica. The vacation proved to be peaceful and relaxing; it gave him a chance to turn off his high-voltage energy for the first time in a long while.

"On my thirtieth birthday—man, it was like it all washed off me," Murphy recalled. Although he did not make any announcement about his new attitude, those close to him definitely noticed the change. He became much more easygoing and relaxed. For one thing, Murphy realized that he did not continually have to be at the top of his field. Being the hottest star around had been the expectation for him when he began to produce hit after hit in the early 1980s. "I was the best five years ago," he told an interviewer in 1992. "Now I just want to be good, and stay good. And if I can't do stuff, I'll just chill."

8

"THIS GUY IS REALLY, REALLY HEAVY"

PERHAPS WHAT IS most remarkable about Eddie Murphy is the range and depth of his abilities. "He can mimic, he can mime, he can do physical comedy, he can do verbal comedy, and then he'll sit down at the piano that's on the set and play beautifully!" said film director Reginald Hudlin, who worked with Murphy on the June 1992 release *Boomerang*. "Not rock 'n' roll but serious piano. This guy is really, really heavy."

From performing stand-up comedy in concert halls, to writing and singing his own songs on records, to acting in and producing movies, it seems there is little Murphy cannot do. Nor is there any reason why he should put limitations on himself. "I dabble with a lot of forms of expression," he has said, "and that's good for me as an artist."

Murphy did not always take his work as a singer and songwriter as seriously as he does now. Although he had been perfecting his imitations of such entertainers as Al Green, Elvis Presley, Lionel Richie, and Stevie Wonder from the time he began "performing" in the family basement, he produced his first album, *How Could It Be*, as a lark. He figured that if audiences did not like it, he could always laugh off his foray into music by turning it into a joke about himself.

Yet *How Could It Be*, released in September 1985, was anything but a joke. The album's first single,

"I'm a comedian who got into movies," Murphy said. "I started out as a stand-up comedian and that's what I'm most comfortable doing."

"Working with Michael was a great experience," Murphy said of "Remember the Time," a music video set in ancient Egypt and made in 1992. In addition to singer Michael Jackson (right), the video also featured supermodel Iman (left).

"Party All the Time," was written and produced by Murphy's musician pal Rick James, and it promptly became a hit. Stevie Wonder also contributed two songs to the album, and Murphy himself wrote several others, among them "C-O-N Confused" and "My God Is Color Blind." All told, the album was so good that it caught many people—including Murphy's fans and members of the music industry—by surprise.

Murphy's music career did not stop there. In August 1989, Columbia Records released his second pop album, *So Happy*. Three years in the making, it contained a number of love songs with sensual lyrics, including the hit single "Put Your Mouth on Me."

"On my first album," Murphy said, "I involved a lot of great people—Stevie Wonder, Rick James. Basically, I let them direct a lot of the project. On this album, though, I really wanted to take my time and be personally involved on every level to make sure the album really was an 'Eddie Murphy' album in every respect." He made sure it was *his* album by once again writing several of the songs. "I'm serious about music," he said, "and this album should show that to everyone."

It certainly did. Like its predecessor, *So Happy* was successful; the album proved to all doubters that Murphy was a musical force to contend with. "Music started out as a hobby when I was younger," he explained in a 1990 interview. "Right now, because I like doing it, I'm gonna continue. So call it a hobby that's gotten out of control."

By early 1992, Murphy was hard at work on his third all-music album, *Love's Alright*, a phrase that pretty much summed up Murphy's frame of mind. At the same time, he was busy making *Boomerang*, which meant that he was putting in long, grueling days and nights. After rushing into Manhattan to perform in the movie, he would race home at night to put the finishing touches on the album in his Bubble Hill recording studio. The album, scheduled for release in 1993 on the Motown label, contains tunes that are smoother, more melodic than the party music that characterized his first two releases. Among its tunes are "Whatzupwitu?" which features Michael Jackson.

One of the album's songs, "Yeah," was inspired by Murphy's daughter and has been described as a "We Are the World" salute to fatherhood. The song features vocals from such stars as Michael and Janet Jackson, Paul McCartney, Elton John, Stevie Wonder, Julio Iglesias, Patti LaBelle, Luther Vandross, Hammer, Jon Bon Jovi, and Heavy D. Profits from the single are reportedly earmarked for Murphy's latest pet project, the Yeah Foundation, an organization intended to help people from all walks of life who are in need.

In describing "Yeah," Murphy said, "I wanted to do a really positive song, and the word 'yes' is the epitome of positivity. I figured it'd be really cool to do a song where everything was 'yes.' "

Music is obviously a creative release that rewards Murphy in many ways. Even though he has considerable clout in the film industry, he has said that making music gives him much more freedom, presumably because there are no studio bosses looking over his shoulder, waiting to approve the end product. "I just go and do whatever I want to do," he said.

In early 1992, Murphy even played a role in the music video version of Michael Jackson's hit single "Remember the Time" from the pop star's *Dangerous* album. In the video, which recalls the noble African history of black Americans, Murphy played the part of the pharaoh Ramses.

The making of the video came on the heels of Murphy's decision to return to moviemaking and appear in a film that would achieve several goals. Above all, he wanted to make a romantic comedy that would portray blacks as highly successful professionals and that did not drag guns or drugs into the plot. He believed there still were not enough movies being made that showed blacks in a positive light.

Of course, Murphy also wanted to make a film that would be a hit, and he was concerned about turning around his reputation among female moviegoers as a heartless, sometimes mean-spirited ladies' man. It was a reputation that had taken hold a few years earlier, with the release of his taped concerts *Delirious* and *Raw*.

"The Eddie Murphy who was in *Raw* does not exist anymore," he said in a 1992 interview with *GQ*. The powers-that-be at Paramount agreed that he needed a new image—one that would better reflect what he was thinking and feeling. Paramount production president John Goldwyn observed of Murphy, "He felt very strongly that he needed to recapture his female audience—to deal with the perception that he's a misogynist, that he uses profanity, that he's a street figure."

With that in mind, Murphy conceived the story idea for *Boomerang* and teamed up again with his

Coming to America writing team. The plot of *Boomerang* revolved around the character of Marcus Graham, an extremely successful cosmetics marketing executive who is irresistible to most women. Marcus gets his comeuppance, however, when his new boss, Jacqueline, played by Robin Givens (whom Murphy had once dated), refuses to succumb to his wiles. Jacqueline, in fact, ends up treating Murphy's character as inconsiderately as he used to treat his old girlfriends. In the end, Marcus learns his lesson, but not before getting one resounding slap on the face by the woman who really loves him, played by Halle Berry.

As successful as *Boomerang* was in portraying blacks as highly capable professionals, the film made other important contributions. In putting together the movie, Murphy made certain that numerous

Murphy and director Reginald Hudlin take a break from filming Boomerang *in 1992. A departure from Murphy's past motion pictures, it presented a far more polished image of the actor-comedian.*

Carrying his daughter, Bria, on one arm, Murphy holds the Lifetime Achievement Award given to him by the National Association for the Advancement of Colored People during a gala "Salute to Eddie Murphy." The award acknowledged his career success and commitment to the advancement of blacks in the entertainment industry.

blacks were employed on the set: the cast was nearly all black, as were half the crew members; he also worked with a black director-producer team for the first time in his career. In addition, Murphy worked to persuade Paramount to join with the Black Filmmaker Foundation to create 10 paid, behind-the-scenes observer positions. These jobs, which helped train young black men and women in various aspects of movie production, was just one of the ways in which he has worked to help out other talented blacks.

Despite all of Murphy's good intentions, *Boomerang*, which reportedly cost $42 million to make, did not gain as wide an audience as he would have liked. Some critics speculated that he had lost his golden touch. Murphy decided to prove them wrong. In the summer of 1992, he began filming *The Distinguished Gentleman*, a comedy about a con man turned congressman. The movie was released in December and showed the 31-year-old entertainer back in top form.

Murphy's next project is slated to be *Beverly Hills Cop 3*, which is bound to please his loyal fans. Beyond that, he is developing an idea for a Western with an all-star black cast, and he is planning to direct his second movie, about a vampire in Brooklyn. What makes this film unique is that Murphy is writing it with his older brother, Charlie.

In addition, Murphy's film production company, Eddie Murphy Productions, owns the rights to *Fences*, August Wilson's Pulitzer Prize–winning play about the stormy relationship between a former Negro league baseball player and one of his sons. It is rumored that Murphy will appear in the film in a supporting role. All told, this mixture of pending projects suggests that he will continue to make fast-action films and comedies but will also tackle more serious roles.

Today, Murphy remains one of the top five highest-paid actors in Hollywood. His deal with Paramount, negotiated several times over the years, currently pays him approximately $12 million per movie, plus approximately 15 percent of the gross earnings (the amount of money a movie makes before expenses are subtracted).

But Murphy will not confine his work to film. In spite of talk that he had retired from the stage, Murphy announced that he plans to return to his first love—stand-up comedy—in the summer of 1993. The tour will be a blend of music and comedy, giving him a chance to showcase his considerable talents.

How Murphy will continue to shape his career remains to be seen—he is only in his early thirties. He still has many years left as a creative artist. "Let's put it this way," Murphy says. "Judge a person by *all* his or her accomplishments. You don't know what I've got planned; you don't know how much money I've given to what organizations and what I want to do, or what my *overall* view is of what I have to do as a black man in this country. So don't sit around and judge me. Don't say, 'Go now, Ed,' . . . I'll go when I'm ready to go! I'll say something when I'm ready to say it!"

And whatever Murphy says, surely his legions of fans will be listening. "I'll never stand on no apple box," he told *Premiere* in 1992. "I'm a cat born in Brooklyn, twelfth-grade education—a regular cat. And I put all my energy into being successful in this business, and that's what happened. . . . The political statement I'm making is that through accomplishments, I'm showing a younger person that he can aspire to be anything."

APPENDIX: THE FILMS AND ALBUMS OF EDDIE MURPHY

FILMS

1982 *48 HRS*
1983 *Trading Places; Delirious*
1984 *Best Defense; Beverly Hills Cop*
1986 *The Golden Child*
1987 *Beverly Hills Cop 2; Raw*
1988 *Coming to America*
1989 *Harlem Nights*
1990 *Another 48 HRS*
1992 *Boomerang; The Distinguished Gentleman*

ALBUMS

1982 *Eddie Murphy*
1983 *Eddie Murphy: Comedian*
1985 *How Could It Be?*
1989 *So Happy*
1993 *Love's Alright*

CHRONOLOGY

————— •❦• —————

1961   Born Edward Regan Murphy on April 3 in Brooklyn, New York

1976   First performs in nightclubs on Long Island

1980   Cast as a featured player on "Saturday Night Live"

1982   Records first comedy album, *Eddie Murphy*; appears in first feature film, *48 HRS*

1983   Stars in *Trading Places*; receives NAACP Image Award for Best Actor in a Motion Picture; signs exclusive contract with Paramount Pictures; Eddie Murphy Productions is formed; Murphy makes HBO special, *Delirious*, later released on videocassette; wins first Grammy Award for comedy album, *Eddie Murphy: Comedian*; leaves "Saturday Night Live" at end of season

1984   Appears in *Best Defense*; receives top billing for first time in *Beverly Hills Cop*

1985   Releases first all-music album, *How Could It Be?*

1986   Stars in *The Golden Child*

1987   Stars in *Beverly Hills Cop 2*; appears in concert film, *Raw*, later released on videocassette

1988   Presents Oscar for Best Picture at Academy Awards ceremony; stars in *Coming to America*; signs deal with CBS-TV to create Eddie Murphy Television Enterprises

1989   Writes, produces, directs, and stars in *Harlem Nights*; releases second all-music album, *So Happy*; daughter, Bria Liana, is born

1990   Murphy stars in *Another 48 HRS*; assumes chairmanship of Paramount / Eddie Murphy Fellowship

1991   Receives NAACP Lifetime Achievement Award

1992   Named the first NATO/ShoWest Star of the Decade; stars in *Boomerang* and *The Distinguished Gentleman*; son, Miles Mitchell, is born

1993   Releases third all-music album, *Love's Alright*

FURTHER READING

Davis, Judith. *The Unofficial Eddie Murphy Scrapbook.* New York: New American Library, 1984.

Eichhorn, Dennis P. *Murphy.* Seattle: Truman Publishers, 1987.

Gross, Edward. *The Films of Eddie Murphy.* Las Vegas: Pioneer Books, 1990.

Hill, Doug, and Jeff Weingrad. *Saturday Night: A Backstage History of "Saturday Night Live."* New York: Vintage, 1987.

Koenig, Teresa, and Rivian Bell. *Eddie Murphy.* Minneapolis: Lerner Publications, 1985.

Marc, David. *Comic Visions: Television Comedy and American Culture.* Boston: Unwin Hyman, 1989.

Null, Gary. *Black Hollywood: The Black Performers in Motion Pictures.* Secaucus, NJ: Citadel, 1975.

Partridge, Marianne, ed. *Rolling Stone Visits "Saturday Night Live."* Garden City, NY: Dolphin Books, 1979.

Ruuth, Marianne. *Eddie: Eddie Murphy from A to Z.* Los Angeles: Holloway House, 1985.

INDEX

PICTURE CREDITS

——— ❦ ———

DEBORAH A. WILBURN is a New York City–based magazine editor and journalist who has written for various national publications. She is currently a senior editor at *Working Mother* magazine.

NATHAN IRVIN HUGGINS, one of America's leading scholars in the field of black studies, helped select the titles for the BLACK AMERICANS OF ACHIEVEMENT series, for which he also served as senior consulting editor. He was the W.E.B. Du Bois Professor of History and of Afro-American Studies at Harvard University and the director of the W.E.B. Du Bois Institute for Afro-American Research at Harvard. He received his doctorate from Harvard in 1962 and returned there as a professor in 1980 after teaching at Columbia University, the University of Massachusetts, Lake Forest College, and the California State University, Long Beach. He was the author of four books and dozens of articles, including *Black Odyssey: The Afro-American Ordeal in Slavery*, *The Harlem Renaissance*, and *Slave and Citizen: The Life of Frederick Douglass*, and was associated with the Children's Television Workshop, National Public Radio, the Boston Athenaeum, the Museum of Afro-American History, the Howard Thurman Educational Trust, and Upward Bound. Professor Huggins died in 1989, at the age of 62, in Cambridge, Massachusetts.